Walking On The Ceiling

Walking On The Ceiling

Norm Sawyer

ISBN 13: 99781988226460
ISBN 10: 1-988226-46-5

Cover Art by Kane Sawyer
Front Cover graphics by Lee MacLennan
Photography by Norm Sawyer

Published by

First Page Solutions
Kelowna, BC, Canada

DEDICATION

This book is dedicated to my mother Margaret. The youngest person I know.

CONTENTS

FOREWORD

As part of my preparation for ministry, I attended an intensive year of Biblical training in which 'Sir Norm' was a key figure. His depth of insight into the written counsel of God challenged (and continues to challenge) me to put hands and feet on my faith in new ways. I can't help but wish I could have a 'faith do-over'…to have another shot to get it right.

He has become, in many ways, my spiritual father. To this day I affectionately and respectfully refer to him as 'Pops' despite the nearness in our age. There is never a meeting, no matter how brief, in which I don't leave richer than before.

Yes, what he has to say is that good.

There is a danger that you will just read this book. I encourage you to chew on it, to turn it over in your mind and heart. There is no way that having read this book that you won't leave richer than before.

Blue Collar Faith.

Pat Hayden

Some days it seems as if common sense has vacated the planet. It is during these times when I need a reminder that there is a God who's got a handle on this planet, He's in control, and it will all be well. One of the ways I remind myself of this truth is through the writings of Norm Sawyer, or as I like to call "Sir Norm".

He is a person that talks the talk and walks the walk, then writes it down in good ol' black and white. Let me tell you, it is good stuff. His "tell it like it is" approach nourishes, corrects, and edifies the soul.

I have greatly benefited from his writings. He tackles tough topics and shares his experiences with transparency which makes him a relatable author. Reading his books is like having your own personal life coach, offering concrete, bible based truth. Read it, apply it, you'll be better for it.

Thank you, Sir Norm.

Toni Lyons

For me, Norm is a teacher, a mentor, an artist, and a friend. He has a gift of taking complex subjects and showing you how to apply them to your everyday life. He is the first to encourage you and the last to give up on you.

True to his signature teaching style, Norm's books are straight to the point and backed by example. His books are filled with foundation life lessons forged through personal experience.

Everyone needs a Norm in their life and if you don't, well at least you have this book.

Norm, thank you for your bulldog tenacity and for sharing your hard-won lessons in this book.

Carolyn Larrett

PART ONE:

HARD CHANGES

The newer padlock on an old door reminded me of something new introduced to the old. Sometimes change is hard when God asks us to do His will. Change is part of growth.

WALKING ON THE CEILING

Proverbs 17:9 Love prospers when a fault is forgiven, but dwelling on it separates close friends.

It is said, "When we forgive, we don't change the past, we change the future." We cannot undo the effects of hurtful things that were said. We cannot undo things that we did or were done to us. We cannot undo things we have seen that should never have been looked at. We can only go forward with a repentant heart and a Godly willingness within our hearts to be who we were made to be in Christ. Phil. 3:13 **Brothers, I do not consider myself yet to have laid hold of it. But one thing I do: Forgetting what is behind and straining toward what is ahead,** 14 **I press on toward the goal for the prize of the upward calling of God in Christ Jesus.**

When our world is upside-down because of past hurts or infected memories, finding our way forward may be difficult. Feelings of being out of place and not quite where we are supposed to be in our heart may run rampant within our entire being. We might even feel like we are walking on the ceiling. Gravity and natural laws seem to be contrary to our ability to grasp where we are and where we are going. Psalm 73:14 **I get nothing but trouble all day long; every morning brings me pain.**

Confusion can become a default setting in our life to the point that we no longer know which way is up or down. Psalm 43:5a **Why, my soul, are you so dejected? Why are you in such turmoil?** It might be time for complete capitulation and ceasing to resist the working of the Holy Spirit within our mind, soul, and body. Some might say, "It is time to get back to basics," but it most likely will be a deeper work than that.

When Joseph finally came to the place of surrender within his heart where he forgave his brothers for the betrayal they had orchestrated upon him by selling him into slavery - the decision to forgive was gut-wrenching. It was so deep a work within Joseph that his world had turned upside-down. The whole palace knew a monumental shift had happened, as the effect of this forgiveness could be heard throughout the palace. Gen. 45:2

He wept loudly; the Egyptians heard it and Pharaoh's household heard about it.

This grace of forgiving not only changed Joseph's future, but also the future of his brothers, father, and eventually a nation. By forgiving the past, Joseph was able to see his own sons blessed by his father. Gen. 48:8 **Then Jacob looked over at the two boys. "Are these your sons?" he asked.** 9 **"Yes," Joseph told him, "these are the sons God has given me here in Egypt." And Jacob said, "Bring them closer to me, so I can bless them."** Forgiveness cleared the way for Joseph to see the blessings of the Lord restore his soul and family.

The majority of wounds that cause festering anger within people are most often caused by acquaintances or family members. These so-called friends and relatives brought hurts, rejections, and sometimes brutality that caused mental, physical, and emotional scars that can become infected. The only balm and ointment that can clean the pustulant stench festering in every part of a person's life is forgiveness. Forgive - and you will be set free!

When Jesus was nailed to the cross and

every injustice committed against Him had been performed with malice, He changed the entire future of the world with these words, "Father, forgive them." Because of the Lord's forgiveness toward us, we walk in grace and the blessing of the Holy Spirit. Who or what must you forgive to be able to stop walking on the ceiling and be set free? We cannot undo the past, but we can change the future. It is our choice. Do it, forgive.

UNEQUALLY YOKED

Proverbs 21:2 Every way of a man is right in his own eyes: but the LORD ponders the hearts.

Everyone has their favorite bible verse that often helps determine their personal persona, drive, and beacon. The one that guides me often is Amos 3:3 **Can two walk together, except they be agreed?** This is a question I ask myself, in most cases, when hard decisions have to be made. Will God and I be on the same page if I go ahead with this plan? Will God and I still be yoked, and will I be walking in the peace of the Lord after I act on the said decision?

I use this bible verse as one of my guardrails and plumb lines in helping me walk the walk Christ inspires in my life. I like this verse because it is simple in explanation. The question asked in the verse answers a lot of the guesswork that comes up in my life. Another way to interpret this verse is by asking, "Will God agree with this?"

A common question today among young people who are looking for a life mate is

"Should I, or do you think God would be OK with me marrying this person?" As I am not a matchmaker, I can only ask the question, "Are you both equally yoked?" 2Cor. 6:14 **Be ye not unequally yoked together with unbelievers: for what fellowship hath righteousness with unrighteousness? and what communion hath light with darkness?** If you go ahead and marry that person, will you be living in the blessing of God or the dwellings of despair? Will you and your prospective spouse be walking with the Lord together after marriage, or will you be dragging his or her sorry carcass to church?

Please forgive my slight sarcasm as I have seen this movie replayed over and over again in the last thirty-five years in different ministries. I am not saying that marriages do not work when one is serving the Lord and the other wants nothing to do with God. Yes, they love each other and life goes on; however, the number one thing on the heart of one who is serving the Lord is that God would save their spouse. They spend the rest of their lives wanting, wishing, and praying for that blessed event to take place.

Thank God when it occasionally happens,

but more often than not these people end up separated. Many times the parties involved end up mad at God. It is very hard to reason with people who are in love with each other. They have this Teflon covering over their ability to see the potential pitfalls that may be just around the corner of their covenanted commitment. God is either the Lord of all or not at all, and that is also in marriage.

Why does God say in His word to take his yoke? Matt. 11:29 **Take my yoke upon you, and learn of me; for I am meek and lowly in heart: and ye shall find rest unto your souls.** 30 **For my yoke is easy, and my burden is light.** The Lord's yoke might be easy and light, but it is a yoke nonetheless. We still have to wear it and learn how to live our lives in Christ with it so that we are pulling and adjusting as the Lord teaches us to use His yoke for His work and His way.

When a new young bull was to be fitted with a yoke and be taught how to pull, he was paired off with an older bull who already knew how to work and pull. The trained bull, by default of being yoked to the young one, would train the young one how to pull without the yoke chafing and gouging the animal. The young bull, also by default of the yoke, would learn how to work side-by-side with the more experienced bull and the work got done.

In our case, the yoke is easy because Christ Himself is right there beside us going through life. We are step-in-step with our Lord. Therefore, it is not an irksome or chafing experience unless we are pulling in the opposite direction.

Regardless of whether we are looking for a spouse, business partner, or friends to hang out with, we all have to walk circumspect and remember that there are times when we will have to ask ourselves and the Lord if we are unequally yoked. We will have to determine if making a life covenant with an unbeliever is the right move for our eternal life. James 3:11 **Can both freshwater and salt water flow from the same spring?**

As Amos points out so well in Amos 3:3 **Can two walk together, except they be agreed?** The beauty of being human is that we have a free choice to walk through this life with or without listening to God. Micah 6:8 **He hath shewed thee, O man, what is good; and what doth the LORD require of thee, but to do justly, and**

to love mercy, and to walk humbly with thy God? Hopefully, we have learned over the years to do our best to be in agreement with God and obey Him because He is Lord. God bless you all.

HELP! I NEED SOMEBODY

Proverbs 29:23 A man's pride will bring him low, but the humble in spirit will retain honor

♪ ♫(Help!) I need somebody (Help!) ♩Not just anybody (Help!) ♪You know I need someone (Help!)♫

In 1965, through serendipity, John Lennon may not have known that the opening lyrics to the song *Help* might become a cry or even a prayer for many people living in this fractured world today.

I was humming and singing this song the other day. I then realized I was thanking God for all the wonderful things He had done for me when I got to the lines "When I was younger so much younger than today, I never needed anybody's help in any way. But now these days are gone and I'm not so self-assured. Now I find I've changed my mind, I've opened up the doors." I said, "Wow Lord, that is exactly what happened. I opened up the door of my life and you moved in and changed it - you gave me your righteousness." Only God in His mercy could have helped me that way. Psalm

109:26 **Help me, O LORD my God: O save me according to thy mercy.**

Help, Lord! What a simple prayer. Psalm 38:22 **Come quickly to help me, my Lord and my Savior.** There is so much truth in the statement that God is faithful. He is the only real help, because He knows our innermost thoughts and intentions of the heart. The Lord intimately knows exactly what kind of help we need. Man's intuition and limited knowledge cannot perceive the depth of our needs; therefore, leaves us wanting, grasping, and needy. Psalm 60:11 **Give us help from trouble, for the help of man is useless.**

Our cry is "Help us, Lord! We are overwhelmed with troubles that are above our ability to overcome. Lord God, the reports of cancer, substance abuse, unnatural obsessions, debilitating anxiety, crushing fears of the unknown, and the inability to trust in anything has stripped us of confidence in ourselves. We need somebody who has overcome all the onslaught, sins, and problems of the world. We need our Savior to step in on our behalf. We need you Lord, a champion who can truly help." Psalm 124:8 **Our help is in the**

name of the LORD, who made heaven and earth. In short - help! It is Godly wisdom at work within us when we call on God for His help.

It does not matter how many years we have walked with our God, there will never be a time we will not need God's help. Why do so many people wait 'til they are having a near-death experience, or they hit the bottom of darkness before humbling themselves and finally praying for help? Psalm 46:1 **God is our refuge and strength, a helper who is always found in times of trouble.**

Why do we wait until we are at the point of being spiritually starved and destitute like the prodigal son before we think of returning home to the Father? Luke 15:17 **When he finally came to his senses, he said to himself, "At home even the hired servants have food enough to spare, and here I am dying of hunger!"** This inability to ask for help is a form of pride. I call it, "The pride of the worm." This pride should not be our default setting. Asking God for help should be a normal daily request that comes genuinely out of our heart.

Help! I need somebody, and that somebody is the Lord Jesus. Jesus is the only honest, true, and reliable help we have in this life. Can man bring assistance and lighten our burdens and difficulties in life? Yes. However, there is no other supernatural help out there for the needs of our soul other than from the Lord Jesus. Acts 4:12 **Salvation exists in no one else, for there is no other name under heaven given to men by which we must be saved.**

Heavenly Father, help us all recognize that you have all the answers for our life - now and forevermore. Help us not be ashamed or reluctant to call on your goodness for help. Jer. 33:3 **Call unto me, and I will answer you, and shew you great and mighty things, which you know not.** We need your help Lord. Amen.

WHAT DO I DO?

Proverbs 24:14 So shall the knowledge of wisdom be unto thy soul: when thou hast found it, then there shall be a reward, and thy expectation shall not be cut off.

I have been in quite a few conversations lately with people who have been struggling with their faith and have said things like, "I just don't know what to do. I'm not sure what God wants of me. I can't seem to get what God is trying to say to me. I'm supposed to know the Lord's voice, but I can't hear Him for the noise in my life. What do I do? I think God has disowned me. I think I have lost my salvation. I cannot feel God's love. I feel like heaven is laughing at me and I'm just a punchline to some holy joke." That last one got to me personally. I was lost for words for this very hurt and bruised person.

I reckon I could have stated some of the standard platitudes, but I felt I would have been disingenuous because I have had some of the same questions in my own heart. I realised that these thoughts and feelings are a battle for our faith. 1Tim. 6:12 **Fight the good fight of faith, lay hold on eternal life, whereunto thou art also called, and hast professed a good profession before many witnesses.**

We will come through these doubts, frustrations, and tribulations. John 16:33 **These things I have spoken unto you, that in me ye might have peace. In the world ye shall have tribulation: but be of good cheer; I have overcome the world.**

During these dry times the last thing anyone wants to hear is "Let go and let God," or, this one always gets me, "God is trying to teach you something, brother." Am I that pathetic of a person that I just never get what God is trying to teach me?

The Psalmist is going through a rough time of doubting and says in Psalm 73:16 **When I thought to know this, it was too painful for me.** Thank God for His written word we can lean into during these times of shaky faith.

During difficult times I think of what Peter said when I am going through my spiritual uncertainty. John 21:3 **Simon Peter saith unto them, "I go**

a fishing." They say unto him, "We also go with thee." They went forth, and entered into a ship immediately; and that night they caught nothing. Here are some well-seasoned disciples who were asking the same questions after Jesus was absent from their presence.

Peter had a family to take care of. All he could think of doing was what he knew. When you don't know what to do, do what you know. Christ is the great Shepherd, He will come and find you.

The next day Jesus is on the seashore with a fire of coals, with fish cooking. John 21:12 **Jesus saith unto them, "Come and dine." And none of the disciples durst ask him, "Who art thou?" knowing that it was the Lord.** Jesus came looking for His disciples and that is the peace we can have in Christ, knowing that the Lord will find us and bring us back on the path of righteousness. This is a great comfort during times of battle and doubt.

Judges 6:13 **And Gideon said unto him, "Oh my Lord, if the LORD be with us, why then is all this befallen us? and where be all his miracles which our fathers told us of, saying, Did not the LORD bring us up from**

Egypt? but now the LORD hath forsaken us, and delivered us into the hands of the Midianites." Gideon gets to the point of what is on his heart. If the LORD is with us, then why is all this rubbish happening in our lives? Why have I not had a prayer answered in ages?

If God is with me, then why does everything I touch turn to garbage? I've named it and claimed it. I've read five steps to receiving, ten steps to getting, and taken another twelve steps just to make sure - and nothing works. What's with that? If God is for me, then why are things the way they are? Gideon had a good question. If we are honest, we have been asking the same thing in our own lives.

The LORD says to Gideon in Judges 6:16 **"Surely I will be with thee, and thou shalt smite the Midianites as one man."** My faith is built up with this story in that God came looking for Gideon. There was nothing special about Gideon's family. Judges 6:14 **And he said unto him, "Oh my Lord, wherewith shall I save Israel? behold, my family is poor in Manasseh, and I am the least in my father's house."**

Gideon says, "I'm the least in this family." Yet

God found him working in fear and doubting his salvation and purpose. However, God found Gideon doing what he knew to get by with what he had, and God met his needs and turned him into a leader.

My admonishment to the readers of this book is - do what you know and trust God will come and find you right where you are. He will love you fully right there, warts and all. 2Cor. 5:17 **Therefore if any man be in Christ, he is a new creature: old things are passed away; behold, all things are become new.**

Judy Garland said, "Always be a first rate version of yourself, instead of a second rate version of someone else." God has made you who you are. There is no one else like you. God knows our address and what our needs are right now. Let Him find us trusting in Him. In Jesus name, I pray this verse over everyone who reads this. Eph. 3:20 **Now all glory to God, who is able, through his mighty power at work within us, to accomplish infinitely more than we might ask or think.** Amen!

THE HUMAN SPILLAGE

Proverbs 14:5 A faithful witness will not lie: but a false witness will utter lies.

Joel Osteen said, "Don't make permanent decisions on temporary feelings."

When we look all around us and see the human spillage that is polluting the earth, air, and waters that we need to live in - we can only wonder how we have made it this far without blowing up the entire world. This same polluting attitude and resulting uncertainties have spilled into the spiritual lives of people worldwide. 2Tim. 4:3 **For the time will come when people will not put up with sound doctrine. Instead, to suit their own desires, they will gather around them a great number of teachers to say what their itching ears want to hear.**

The Messiah syndrome - as in we need a Superman from another galaxy to save us - is rampant with people claiming to have found the way to deliverance from all the mayhem that is about to come upon mankind. Whether for spiritual growth or for daily living, people are looking for some kind of Messiah to save their solipsistic existence. Matt. 24:5 **For many will come in my name, saying, 'I am the Christ,' and they will lead many astray.**

The pendulum swings of belief are so incredibly vast and wide that people feel forced to make decisions at a rapid speed. They feel caught up in the momentum of multiple choices of ideas and beliefs that are dangling before their hearts on a continual basis. The human spillage has created a feeble condition that has reached a tipping point of worldwide saturation that people are having a hard time hearing a clear and honest message. Matt 24:23 **At that time, if anyone says to you, 'Look, here is the Christ!' or 'There He is,' do not believe it.**

The Lord warned us that these days would come and sin would increase in intensity as the end times approached. His encouraging word to us who walk in Christ was straightforward. He said to keep your peace that you have in the Lord and make your life decisions based on His word and not what you see going on around the earth. John 16:33 **These things I have spoken to you, so**

that in Me you may have peace. In the world you have tribulation, but take courage; I have overcome the world. God also admonished us to stay faithful and continue to trust in Him. Prov. 3:5 **Trust in the LORD with all your heart and lean not on your own understanding;** 6 **in all your ways submit to him, and he will make your paths straight.**

The human condition is manifesting such cravings and needs for personal identity and fulfillment that anything seems to be accepted and eaten up with ravenous gluttony. If you have the Lord's peace in your life and heart, then it is easier to shun the multiple snake oil cures offered as true salvation. However, if you are desperate in heart, soul, and mind then anything goes. Prov. 27:7 **A person who is full refuses honey, but even bitter food tastes sweet to the hungry.**

How badly can humanity corrupt its life? We know from history past that God endured to the point where He said it was enough. The heart of man was exhibiting corruption beyond understanding and had reached a dreadful saturation point of evil. Gen. 6:5 **And GOD saw that the wickedness of man was great**

in the earth, and that every imagination of the thoughts of his heart was only evil continually. Will it get that bad again? I do not know, but some say we are there already.

We can be encouraged that grace is at work in the dispensation that we are living in today. Rom. 5:20 **God's law was given so that all people could see how sinful they were. But as people sinned more and more, God's wonderful grace became more abundant.** 21 **So just as sin ruled over all people and brought them to death, now God's wonderful grace rules instead, giving us right standing with God and resulting in eternal life through Jesus Christ our Lord.**

We do have the advantage of the finished work of the cross and the blood of Jesus at work in our hearts and lives. The generation before the flood did not have that blessing working in their hearts. However, we do. So as we look around and see the human spillage affecting the world, let us keep making our permanent decisions based on the leading of the Holy Spirit and not the noise in the streets. Blessings and peace to us all.

FUNCTIONING IN DYSFUNCTION

Proverbs 5:13 I have not obeyed the voice of my teachers, nor inclined my ear to those who instructed me!

Good enough is not God's best. Close enough is not that close. When we are living from one bad situation to another and become comfortable functioning in the dysfunctions of life, our spiritual ear can become dull of hearing what the Lord is saying to our soul. We no longer try to understand what God is saying in our lives. Heb. 5:11 **We have much to say about this, but it is hard to make it clear to you because you no longer try to understand.**

St Augustine said: "You are what you love." If you love chaos and are constantly operating from a point of dysfunction, then your heart becomes slow to grasp what God is sowing into your heart. Fear starts to replace faith and as someone said: "Fear tolerated is faith contaminated."

There seems to be a nonchalance or norm about the dysfunction that consumes most of the day's events. People are learning to function within their dysfunction, then they wonder why nothing of eternal value is getting done or realized in their hearts.

They put stronger efforts into doing the same dysfunctional things and end up angry and discouraged with life. Hag. 1:6 **You have sown much, and harvested little. You eat, but you never have enough; you drink, but you never have your fill. You clothe yourselves, but no one is warm. And he who earns wages does so to put them into a bag with holes.**

People are tiredly rushing here and there, only to put another temporary patch on a family argument or blunder through another day of endless tasks to get blindsided by an unexpected bill that empties the family savings account; bringing unnatural pressures to the continual everyday dysfunction.

Some want to pull their hair out and scream something outrageous or shout: "Stop the madness." Prov. 5:13 **I have not obeyed the voice of my teachers, Nor inclined my ear to those who instructed me!** Others simply fold over in exhaustion. Psalm 6:6 **I am weary from my**

groaning. Every night my couch is drenched with tears, my bed is soaked through.

Dysfunction is not God's plan for our lives. Chaos is not God's design for a life of peace in Christ. Poor health because of stress is not God's purpose for our relationship with the Lord on this earth. Jesus came that we would have, possess, own, and exist in and with an abundant life. John 10:10 **The thief comes not, but for to steal, and to kill, and to destroy: I am come that they might have life, and that they might have it more abundantly.**

God's love for us is real and abundant. His thoughts towards us are thoughts of victory and blessing, not second-hand existence. I reiterate what I have said in the past. The enemy of our soul tries to keep us focused on the regrets of the past and the fears of the future, so that we do nothing for God today. Psalm 118:24 **This is the day the Lord has made; We will rejoice and be glad in it.**

God wants us focused on the day we are in, because that is the day we are actually living. The past has passed and the future is not here yet. Today is the day of living and salvation. Today is the day to function in the rest, peace, and joy of the Lord. Today is the day to incline our ear to the teaching of the Lord. Today, look up and bless the Lord. Psalm 46:10a **Be still, and know that I am God.** Stop the momentum of a dysfunctional life by functioning in the love of God for this day. May the peace of God favor us this day. Amen!

BURNED OUT ON RELIGION

Proverbs 14:12 There is a way that seems right to a person, but its end is the way to death.

What has been done and what is being done in the name of religion has disillusioned a generation of people. The nastiness that religion can cause in people is horrific. Just before a fanatic detonates the explosives strapped to his or her body, they are heard to say, "God is great." Well, yes, God is great, but His law is love. John 3:16 **For God so loved the world, that he gave his only begotten Son, that whosoever believes in him should not perish, but have everlasting life.** God promotes life, not carnage.

If all a person has in this lifetime is a rote exercise in religious activity without getting close to God Himself, then what good is it? 1Cor. 15:17 **And if Christ has not been raised, then your faith is useless and you are still guilty of your sins.** It is not a religion on its own that fulfills, but a heartfelt relationship with God who gives life and causes us to seek more.

God gave us a risen Lord in Jesus Christ to put our faith in so that we can have an eternal relationship with God the Father. The resurrection of Christ through faith gives us the righteousness and freedom we need to become guilt-free. This is needed so we could live in God's presence and be accepted by Him.

Paul said when writing to the Corinthians, and I'm paraphrasing here, "If all we have in Christ is a feel-good religious activity for this life, then we are more pathetic than the religious fanatics throughout the world." 1Cor. 15:19 **If we have put our hope in Christ for this life only, we should be pitied more than anyone.**

We have a more sure reality than just making it through this life. Because of Christ, we have eternal life. Any sin can be laid on Jesus' blood-stained cross. No matter what sin anyone has ever committed, it can be forgiven. God does not need our permission to forgive. He forgives anyone who asks for it. Rom. 9:15 **For he saith to Moses, "I will have mercy on whom I will have mercy, and I will have compassion on whom I will have compassion."**

Religion on its own does not cleanse us of

our sins. Religion cannot restore nor heal a soul to be at peace with God. Religion without Christ cannot save the lost from the eternal destruction that is to come. If all we end up doing in life is try to balance the bad things with good things done out of our own efforts, then we will get burned out on religion and so will everyone around us. Hag. 1:7 **Thus saith the LORD of hosts; "Consider your ways."**

Religion without Christ is boring, insipid, and hard to stick with. Jesus has given us the Holy Spirit to strengthen us to help us move forward in God and keep growing from glory to glory. We are not just getting better at being religious, we are being transformed from the inside out and becoming what God intended us to be through Christ. 2Cor. 3:18 **And we, who with unveiled faces all reflect the glory of the Lord, are being transformed into His image with intensifying glory, which comes from the Lord, who is the Spirit.** With intensifying glory, and not some repeated mumbling of religious words. There is life-changing power through Christ, and only God can give it to us.

If you are burned out on religion, then ask

Jesus to awaken your heart and mind so that you can live in the joy of the Lord. The joy of the Lord is our strength. With that strength, we can move the mountains in life. With the strength Jesus sowed within us, we can have life and have it more abundantly. When we are in Christ then the Lord's joy, peace, and love will be healing for our whole body, soul, and mind. Prov. 3:8 **This will be healing for your body and strengthening for your bones.** Get out of religious activity and come into a relationship with God our Father. In Jesus name.

WALKING IN SHADOWS

Proverbs 4:18 But the path of the just is as the shining light, that shines more and more unto the perfect day.

I was recently looking at a piece of artwork. Some of the people in the painting were clear and defined, while others were in shadow and silhouetted. I thought of the parallels we see when we accept Christ as Lord. After Jesus enters our heart, we become defined and clear within our soul and rise toward His purpose in life. However, so many people go through life just shadows of what they could be. If only they would let God in, their souls would come alive. Psalm 144:4 **Man is like a breath; his days are like a passing shadow.**

If the Lord is not directing your life, then there is not much you can accomplish that will have eternal value. John 15:5 **I am the vine and you are the branches. The one who remains in Me, and I in him, will bear much fruit. For apart from Me you can do nothing.** Without

Jesus as the Lord of our life, we can only exist in part because we have not been made whole. Jesus came that we have life, and a full one at that. John 10:10b **I am come that they might have life, and that they might have it more abundantly.**

We do not want to walk in the shadows of uncertainty, or live in the darkness of a sinful life. The weight sin puts upon a soul is too great a burden to live with. We were never designed to live in the shadows of darkness and wither away unfulfilled. Psalm 102:11 **My days are like a lengthening shadow, and I wither away like grass.**

Our creator, God, is pure love, righteousness, and light. The light and righteous purity emanating from God is what He wants us to walk in. There is no room for shadows and darkness within God or His eternal plan for us. Our path is clear and bright. Prov. 4:18 **But the path of the just is as the shining light, that shines more and more unto the perfect day.**

Clarity of heart and mind is what the population of the world looks for in all their consuming ways. Day after day they strive to get that thing that will make them superhuman and perfect, but there is no magic potion to drive the shadows within the heart away. A miraculous transformation is needed so that the clear, loving, and pure heart of God comes and lives within our soul. We need a spiritual heart transplant. Only Jesus can do it. John 3:7 **Do not be amazed that I said to you, You must be born again.**

Come out from the shadows and begin to live in the light of God's love and living word. Let God paint you with a clear mandate for your appointed time on earth. Let the Lord rebuild and mould your heart to be the person you were clearly meant to be. 2Cor. 6:17 **Therefore come out from among them and be separate, says the Lord. Touch no unclean thing, and I will receive you.** Bring into the light all the things hidden in the shadows of your life. Allow the love of God to fill your soul with the peace and understanding you have been searching for your whole life. Walk in the light as He is in the light. Amen!

TIRED ON THE INSIDE

Proverbs 4:2 For I give you good doctrine, forsake ye not my law.

Job 10:1 **My soul is weary of my life; I will leave my complaint upon myself; I will speak in the bitterness of my soul.**

My mother has an expression to explain her tiredness. She says, "I am tired on the inside." That normally means she has to go lie down and have a rested sleep and regain her energy for the day. There is a tiredness on the inside that cannot be dismissed with a short nap. It is the weariness of the soul that occurs when someone has tried everything but God to gain peace and stability, but finds none. They have become tired of an empty life with no blessed future on the horizon.

How many people are tired on the inside and like Job says of his soul - he can no longer keep the tired bitterness from coming forth? Many people are good at hiding the emotional war going on inside their soul and with great showmanship are able to display a strong front to the world. This pretense of face-saving can only go so far before the walls will eventually come tumbling down, so to speak.

King Saul had a hard time hiding his jealous heart when it came to David and God's favor on David's life. Saul was so weary and tired on the inside that he needed David to play music to help quell the spirits that oppressed and tormented him. 1Sam. 16:23 **And whenever the tormenting spirit from God troubled Saul, David would play the harp. Then Saul would feel better, and the tormenting spirit would go away.** Even though it was David who helped Saul gain peace - Saul, with hatred in his heart, still attacked David ruthlessly. 1Sam. 19:10 **Saul tried to nail David to the wall with the spear, but he escaped from Saul's presence and the spear drove into the wall. David escaped quickly that night.**

Unless the Lord is your peace, the little peace you have will be temporary and fleeting. Mark 4:25 **For whoever has, more will be given to him, and whoever does not have, even what he has will be taken away from him.**

Many workers in ministry give testimony to

their tiredness on the inside. This sometimes happens when the ministry itself becomes a god and Jesus is left to become a subject of religious conversation and an exercise in weak apologetics. Having lost the real conviction of Jesus, these workers of religion become empty of heart. Jesus is relegated to a side-note preached, rather than the Savior who lives. Phil. 1:15 **To be sure, some preach Christ out of envy and rivalry, but others out of good will.**

God within our being gives life and will quench the thirst that weariness produces. John 7:38 **"He who believes in Me, as the Scripture said, From his innermost being will flow rivers of living water."** If you have become tired on the inside, then it is time to allow the spirit of God that lives within you to fill your soul with life and assurance. Allow the Holy Spirit to fill you with the first love you had when Jesus was everything to you. Prov. 4:2 **For I give you good doctrine, forsake ye not my law.**

Jesus himself asks us to return to our first love for Him. This will heal the tiredness inside. Jesus is Lord, not just a conversation piece. May we all find and keep Him in our hearts. Amen.

FORGIVE YOURSELF

Proverbs 18:14 The spirit of a man will sustain his infirmity; but a wounded spirit who can bear?

Someone said, "You are led by your spirit or your wounds."

Forgive yourself, because God already did. The hardest person to forgive in life is often yourself, because you know your own heart and your own shortcomings. You also know the damage and resulting wounds from the choices you made in life that are now affecting your soul. We make personal judgments about ourselves from the wounded part of our soul, rather than the healed part of our spirit that came by faith.

We have to accept the fact that we are forgiven. There is now no condemnation for ourselves in the same proportion that is available to all the people who have accepted Christ as Lord. Rom. 8:1 **There is therefore now no condemnation to them which are in Christ Jesus, who walk not after the flesh, but after the Spirit.**

I do not know why we are harder on ourselves

than God is, but we often are. I am not sure how the Apostle Paul forgave himself but he did, even with the history of his memories. Paul had been responsible for the death of Christians and carried that knowledge in his heart; however, after Paul had received Christ as his Lord, he goes on to declare that he has wronged no man. 2Cor. 7:2 **Receive us; we have wronged no man, we have corrupted no man, we have defrauded no man.** What allowed Paul to say such a thing when his own history said differently?

The forgiving power of the blood and sacrifice of Jesus was the first thing Paul got a hold of in his heart. The second thing was being able to accept the full redemption of that work within his heart and life. Paul could say by faith - no matter what had happened in his past life or present ministry - to forgive the past and move on to the future by faith was the power of the resurrection of Christ now working in his soul.

He could forget the past and move forward in Christ every new day because he had forgiven himself. Phil. 3:13 **Brothers, I do not consider that I have made it my own. But one thing I do: forgetting what lies behind and straining**

forward to what lies ahead, 14 **I press on to reach the end of the race and receive the heavenly prize for which God, through Christ Jesus, is calling us.**

How we move forward in our Christian walk is largely determined by how we accept the forgiveness of God and apply that forgiveness to our lives. Trusting the finished work of the cross, by faith on our part, is the first step to personal forgiveness and freedom. The word says that we have known and believed the love that God has for us. Might this be the problem? We can believe God loves others, but because we know ourselves we find it hard to believe He could love us.

This is just a tactic the enemy of our soul uses. Satan has used this lie on all people throughout history. The devil is a liar and will always lie to us about the love God has for us. John 8:44b **When he speaks a lie, he speaks of his own: for he is a liar, and the father of it.**

It is time to forgive ourselves of all the things that have wounded us. It is for these very wounds Jesus died on the cross. Our hurts, wounds, sicknesses, and sins of all kinds have been paid in full by the love, blood, and sacrifice Jesus gave us.

It is time to stop being led by the wounds and festering injuries of your past life and allow the healing balm and resurrection power of the Holy Spirit to heal your soul completely. By faith, let us enter into the fullness of grace that was given to every man who accepts the gift of forgiveness. Yes, forgive yourself, and bless the Lord for it. Amen.

PART 1:

QUESTIONS FOR UNDERSTANDING

1. *What did you learn in this section of the book?*
2. *What surprised you the most?*
3. *What subject(s) spoke to your heart?*
4. *Did the material that you read help you understand the subject(s) more or less?*
5. *What topics are important to you? Why?*
6. *How do these articles relate to you?*
7. *After reading this section of the book, what will you change in your life?*

PART TWO:

BEING FREE

Being free means different things to different people. When we remove the clutter from our lives, we are left in a quiet place to commune with our God.

NOT GUILTY

Proverbs 30:10 Don't slander a servant to his master, lest he curse you, and you be held guilty.

We feel guilty because we are guilty! Guilty of slander, guilty pleasures, guilty feelings, guilty plea, guilty sin, and guilty of breaking laws. Whether the laws are spiritual, federal, state, provincial, municipal, or social we are guilty of breaking some law - somehow and somewhere.

People feel guilty because they are guilty of sin. Guilt is their default setting in life and a need to be set free of the guilt is felt deep within, but with no understanding of how to get it done; therefore, they stay guilty as charged. This is why these same people come up with all kinds of self-righteous antics to appease the accusations of guilt that are running wild within their soiled souls. Rom. 7:24 **O wretched man that I am! who shall deliver me from the body of this death?**

How obvious it becomes to those who are in Christ to see the need for a Savior to save and deliver them from their guilt and their personal idea of righteousness. To be pronounced guiltless and sinless by our God because of our faith in the work of the cross and blood of Jesus is an overwhelming blessing within our soul. The peace within our conscience will cause us to bring praises and gratitude to our Lord when we find ourselves resting in the love of God who says we are no longer guilty as charged.

The worldly person cannot see their need for deliverance from their guilt, because their scales of tit for tat in life are rigged in their personal favor at best and warped at worst. Prov. 11:1 **A false balance is an abomination to the LORD, but a just weight is his delight.**

The just weight, in this case, can only be justified through Christ and His finished work of redemption. Only God can remove our guilt through His perfect sacrifice. There is nothing within ourselves that can pull it off. Isa. 43:11 **I, yes I, am the LORD, and apart from me there is no savior.**

If we, as Christians, are going to be held guilty, then let it be for good works and the destruction of the devil's attacks and agendas. Let us not be guilty of slandering our brothers, sisters, and leaders whom the Lord our Master has redeemed. 1Pet. 3:17 **Remember, it is better to suffer for doing good, if that is what God wants, than to suffer for doing wrong!**

We should be proclaiming what Sargent Shriver said when asked about the Peace Corps' enthusiasm. "The Peace Corps is guilty of enthusiasm and a crusading spirit. But we're not apologetic for it." Yes, I will take that humble attitude into my Christian walk with Christ any day. May we all be accused and found guilty of being a blessing in the kingdom of God. May our attitudes be full of enthusiasm and a crusading spirit for helping redeem all man unto God in love.

Guilt and shame can paralyze our growth in the Lord if we do not put all demonic accusations under the blood of Jesus. Feelings of not being good enough, loved, or accepted are not from God. Eph. 1:4 **Even before he made the world, God loved us and chose us in Christ to be holy and without fault in his eyes.** We have been accepted and made righteous through the finished work of the cross and the blood of Jesus.

We have been washed of our guilty sins and the charges that came with sin have also been acquitted. We are made new. The pronouncement of guilt over us is now "Not Guilty." 2Cor. 5:17 **Therefore, if anyone is in Christ, he is a new creation. The old has passed away; behold, the new has come.**

The Apostle Peter was riddled with guilt when he denied knowing Jesus. Luke 22:61 **And the Lord turned and looked at Peter. Then Peter remembered the word the Lord had spoken to him: "Before the rooster crows today, you will deny Me three times."** 62 **And he went outside and wept bitterly**. After the Resurrection of Jesus, He encountered Peter and took away his guilt by restoring Peter's heart and setting him back on the Gospel trail so to speak.

Only Jesus can remove the guilt of sin, because He paid for it in full. Only the Lord can renounce our eternal punishment, because He took that punishment upon Himself. Only God can say we are not guilty, because the guilt was nailed to the cross of Jesus and we are redeemed. What can we say but "Thank you, Lord, for your goodness toward us." Amen.

BE DO HAVE

Proverbs 3:26 For the LORD shall be thy confidence, and shall keep thy foot from being taken.

If only I could have that new car, then I would be able to do this work, then I would be happy. If only I could have that money, then I would buy this thing, then I would be happy. If only, if only, if only I could have!

This world is rotating on an axis of dissatisfaction as we are listening to a constant tune of "If only I could have, then I would do, then I would be!" We have this totally backward.

We were created as human-beings and not human-doings. If I **be** in Christ, then I will know what to **do**, then I will **have** His peace that I am looking for and will not be looking at all the things that are offered as replacements for God Himself. John 15:7 **If ye abide in me, and my words abide in you, ye shall ask what ye will, and it shall be done unto you.**

Clarke's Commentary 1. Be united to Christist -

if ye abide in me. 2. That in order to be preserved in this union, we must have our lives regulated by the doctrine of Christ - and my words abide in you.

If I be united to Christ through the finished work of the cross, I will do His will and have His life ever abounding in me. Prov. 3:26 **For the LORD shall be thy confidence, and shall keep thy foot from being taken.**

I was created to be a son of God in order to do His will so that I could have a relationship with Him eternally. The enemy's agenda for our soul is to sow dissatisfaction and yearning for anything other than a pure relationship with Christ our Lord. John 10:10 **The thief comes not, but for to steal, and to kill, and to destroy: I am come that they might have life, and that they might have it more abundantly.**

If I just be in Christ, then my soul's compass will always point to His will and I will have His guidance to get there.

HOLY AND WHOLLY FORGIVEN

Proverbs 9:10 The fear of the LORD is the beginning of wisdom, and the knowledge of the Holy One is understanding.

Hebrews 8:12 **For I will be merciful to their unrighteousness, and their sins and their iniquities will I remember no more.**

It's too good to be true. There has got to be a catch. Surely it cannot be that easy to walk in the wholeness and absolute forgiveness of God? How can this be a reality or even true? I am so sinful and continually fall to the cravings of every kind. God must be mad at me because I once did something wrong. Can God love and forgive a person like me?

Unfortunately, this is the human response to God's grace, because His forgiveness is free and given from a position of pure love. The graceful forgiveness of God is just that - full of grace. Forgiveness comes to those who accept it by faith and receive the cleansing power it has for our soul. There are no antics to perform or mountains to climb to earn God's forgiveness. It truly is a pure and honest gift. Eph. 2:8 **For by grace you have been saved through faith. And this is not your own doing; it is the gift of God,** 9 **not a result of works, so that no one may boast.**

I once heard someone describe what they felt like when they had finally accepted God's forgiveness. They said, "It felt like a warm bath of forgiveness." Wow, what an image of soaking in the warmth of God's love and holy blessings. Talk about being washed in the blood of the Lamb and coming out clean. 1John 1:7 **But if we walk in the light, as he is in the light, we have fellowship with one another, and the blood of Jesus his Son cleanses us from all sin.**

It is hard to comprehend this kind of love that God has for us, because the world is so full of deception and lies that when real truth like God's love comes along it becomes suspect. Our human default position is sin-mindedness. A righteous-mindedness can only come through the regeneration of Christ's work and sacrifice. Jesus offered Himself for us to procure an eternal work in our hearts. It must be done by God Himself so that it actually works. Our salvation was and still is God's idea. Rom. 5:8 **But God proves His love for us in this: While we were still sinners, Christ died for us.**

How can we understand the knowledge of the Holy One as the Proverb says, if we do not have the indwelling of the Holy One within us? The rebirth and regeneration of our soul gives us the right standing we need to be in fellowship with our heavenly Father. Wow! We have the right to stand before God and with our God because of what Jesus did for us. We are holy and wholly forgiven. Eph. 1:7 **In Him we have redemption through His blood, the forgiveness of sins,** 8 **according to the riches of His grace which He made to abound toward us in all wisdom and prudence.**

Yes, soaking in the warm bath of forgiveness brings life to our soul, mind, and body. What an eternal gift God's salvation has turned out to be. No wonder the word of God says the devil would never have provoked the crucifixion of Jesus had he known what the end result would be for mankind. 1Cor. 2:8 **None of the rulers of this world understood it, because if they had, they would not have crucified the Lord**

of glory.

Our salvation is Holy inspired. All we have to do is receive this gift of forgiveness wholly within our heart. Thank you, Lord, for your love that is of eternal worth. Thank you for your eternal plan and that you saw us in it. Jer. 1:5a **I chose you before I formed you in the womb; I set you apart before you were born.**

IT'S ASSURANCE, NOT INSURANCE

Proverbs 15:25 The way of life is above to the wise, that he may depart from hell beneath.

We live in an over-legislated land and country. "There ought to be a law," someone says, and in no time there is. Soon, we will have to wear a helmet to walk down the sidewalk because someone, somewhere, will fall down and crack their skull. I hope not, on both counts!

In the same way, we cannot legislate holiness, we cannot legislate a risk-free life. Go ahead and buy some insurance to take care of the needs of family and friends. Continue to look for ways to minimize the risk of maiming and crippling one's self in a workplace or a home environment, as this is wisdom.

However, when it comes to our soul, it is a blessed assurance of real life and not an insurance that nothing will ever go wrong. Acts 17:31 **Because He hath appointed a day, in the which He will judge the world in righteousness by that man whom He hath ordained; whereof**

He hath given assurance unto all men, in that He hath raised him from the dead.

A no-risk life is not possible. As my friend Scott says, "We only have to look to God the Father to see the biggest risk ever taken and that was the creation of man." With full assurance in God's heart, He created a human being in His image with a free-will and ability of choice to choose God and His love for mankind. Gen. 1:27 **So God created man in his own image, in the image of God created he him; male and female created he them.** Now that was a risk!

I do believe in divine protection, health, provision, and guidance. I try to live my life in the assurance of God's love and leading so that I can maneuver my way through the maze and warrens of this precarious world. I also know many of you are doing the same thing, but life happens and it comes and tests our hearts with hard to extreme battles that can weary our souls.

Isa. 40:30 **Even the youths shall faint and be weary, and the young men shall utterly fall:**
31 **But they that wait upon the LORD shall renew their strength; they shall mount up with wings as eagles; they shall run, and not**

be weary; and they shall walk, and not faint. What is it that gets us through these hard times? Is it the fact that we have an insurance policy with God? No! It is the fact that we have a blessed assurance of His power and love working in our souls and on our behalf for the glory of His love and purpose in our lives.

It is the assurance that God has blessed us with something more sure than insurance. Insurance runs out and has to be renewed. Often times the premiums become cost prohibitive, but not the assurance of the Holy Spirit. His eternal and caressive assurance runs forever and is able to sustain us through the darkest valleys until we are lifted into the highest of highs. Heb. 6:11 **And we desire that every one of you do shew the same diligence to the full assurance of hope unto the end.**

Abraham and Sarah took a risk when they went out from the land of their fathers to find a city whose builder was God. Heb. 11:8 **By faith Abraham, when he was called to go out into a place which he should after receive for an inheritance, obeyed; and he went out, not knowing whither he went.** They took a risk by leaving their homeland, received a child of promise, and became the parents of many nations.

Jacob took a risk by allowing his son Benjamin to go with his brothers to Egypt for food during a famine. Gen. 43:13 **Take also your brother, and arise, go again unto the man:** 14 **And God Almighty give you mercy before the man, that he may send away your other brother, and Benjamin. If I be bereaved of my children, I am bereaved.** Jacob took a risk with his son Benjamin and blessings of blessings received Joseph who was thought to be dead because of a harmful ruse played on Jacob. Gen. 46:4 **I will go down with thee into Egypt; and I will also surely bring thee up again: and Joseph shall put his hand upon thine eyes.**

Daniel took a risk praying to his God openly when a law had been enforced that King Darius was the only one to be given homage to. Dan. 6:7 **All the presidents of the kingdom, the governors, and the princes, the counsellors, and the captains, have consulted together to establish a royal statute, and to make a firm decree, that whosoever shall ask a petition of any God or man for thirty days, save of thee,**

O king, he shall be cast into the den of lions.

Daniel took a risk in his God and the result was a declaration from the same king that Daniel's God was God and there were none like Him. Dan. 6:26 **I make a decree, That in every dominion of my kingdom men tremble and fear before the God of Daniel: for he is the living God, and steadfast for ever, and his kingdom that which shall not be destroyed, and his dominion shall be even unto the end.**

Paul took a risk preaching the gospel of Jesus Christ and was beaten for it. 2Cor. 11:25 **Thrice was I beaten with rods, once was I stoned, thrice I suffered shipwreck, a night and a day I have been in the deep.** Paul took a risk, and because he did we have most of the New Testament at our fingertips whenever we want to read and believe the assurance of our loving God.

The gospel is the power of Christ living within each one of us who have received Him as Lord. Rom. 1:16 **For I am not ashamed of the gospel of Christ: for it is the power of God unto salvation to every one that believes; to the Jew first, and also to the Greek.** Thank God Paul took that risk in God, and thank God that God took that risk in Paul.

There will never be a risk-free life, but we can have a blessed assurance in the life that has risk in it. Whenever we take a faith-filled risk in the Lord our God, then the assurance of hope in Him will bring us into righteous victory and blessing beyond that which we can ask or think. Isa. 32:17 **And the work of righteousness shall be peace; and the effect of righteousness quietness and assurance for ever.**

OCTOBER ROSES

Proverbs 31:21 She is not afraid of the snow for her household: for all her household are clothed with scarlet.

The passing of Indian summer announced its end as the last and faded pink blooms struggled to give a display of summer strength. October nights ushered in the chill and frost that foretells the inevitable arrival of winter. Rose bushes supporting their final seasonal blooms whispered a message within me, resulting in one of life's lessons that can be gleaned when one stops and smells the roses.

I considered the struggles and obstacles that October roses encounter in their daily attempt at existence. Its nemesis of changing temperatures and frequent northerly wind gusts take its daily toll on this flower of romantic intention. The end of their growing season is inevitable, yet these flowers persist in expressing their velvet charm and pastel beauty until the final petal drops.

This floral expression of survival instills a

notion within me, in that I have had the privilege of knowing people whose backbone and character were made of the same persistent integrity and spine for living. Phil. 4:13 **I can do all things through Christ who strengthens me.**

We all know people who in the face of insurmountable odds overcame their fiercest battle and still held the integrity of God in their hearts. Like October roses these saints continued to bloom and express what Christ had put in their hearts, no matter what their season looked like on the inevitable horizon.

We can all name a person who brought us a delivering word, help, or an answer to a situation in our life. At that moment they were an answer to prayer, yet they themselves were struggling with their own major issues. Like October roses their hearts bloomed large because Christ is the Lord of their heart. Eph. 3:20 **Now all glory to God, who is able, through his mighty power at work within us, to accomplish infinitely more than we might ask or think.**

We read and hear of great acts of courage that take place in written accounts in the bible. David and Goliath. Moses at the Red Sea. Samson warring with the jawbone of a donkey. Elisha on Mount Carmel. Stephen sentenced to death for his faith and praising God as the mob killed him. These incredible acts of courage are ours to build our faith upon through God who made these miracles happen.

But what about you and me, the everyday person walking out our faith in Christ? Do we have this courage within us? I believe we do, because we have all seen it played out in less dramatic forms every day in the saints we walk with. We just have to stop and smell the roses, per se, to see it.

These October roses continue to bloom and are not afraid of the next season of their life, no matter what battle is confronting them. Phil. 3:13 **Brothers and sisters, I do not consider myself yet to have taken hold of it. But one thing I do: Forgetting what is behind and straining toward what is ahead.** Stand up and push forth a display of spiritual strength in the face of your north wind. Bloom where God has planted you in Christ.

Take the time this week and stop and look at the roses put on their final display. Think of whose courage these roses remind you of. Take a moment and thank God for that person and pray a blessing over them. Eph. 6:18 **Pray in the Spirit at all times and on every occasion. Stay alert and be persistent in your prayers for all believers everywhere.** Be strong in the Lord. Our next season is upon us. Blessings.

HAPPY IS THAT MAN

Proverbs 3:13 Happy is the man that finds wisdom, and the man that gets understanding.

Robert Breault said, “Be happy and a reason will come along.”

We all have our own thoughts on what would make us happy, but God knows and tells us what would really make us happy for the long term. Real happiness starts by being at peace in our own heart and in right standing with our heavenly Father. Psalm 32:1 **Happy are those whose sins are forgiven, whose wrongs are pardoned.**

There is no greater feeling of happiness than knowing in the deepest part of our heart that we are cleansed of our sins and accepted by God. When we know that we know and have no doubt of God’s complete forgiveness that was given to us - we will truly know real happiness. Yes, happy is the man whose sins are forgiven.

When we walk in this realization of sinless happiness, we will be like the saints of old. We will do great exploits in the kingdom of our God.

Dan. 11:32b **But the people that do know their God shall be strong, and do exploits.** When your heart and thoughts are clean because of the work Christ did within you, there will be joy and happiness emanating from your being. You will be a pleasure to be around because that type of happiness is contagious, infectious, and inspiring. The everyday and mundane rote feelings of living will change to a desire to be at peace with God. Psalm 18:29 **With you I can attack a barricade, and with my God I can leap over a wall.**

Another happy person is the man whom God corrects. Job 5:17 **Behold, happy is the man whom God corrects: therefore despise not thou the chastening of the Almighty.** We have been taught throughout our lifetime that failure or being wrong is somehow a shortcoming within our character. This is so far from the truth. How can we ever learn anything unless we are corrected when we get it wrong? Pastor Doug Glada once wrote, "God's correction is not God's rejection." We need God to correct our going and coming so that we remain in the will of God and live a fulfilled life. Jer. 29:11 **For I know the thoughts that I think toward you, saith the LORD,**

thoughts of peace, and not of evil, to give you an expected end.

If airline pilots did not correct their flight patterns along routes to the cities of destination, then most planes would be way off course. Unless a ship's captain follows a navigational chart to the safe harbor that they are headed for, they may become in danger of running unto a reef and wrecking the ship. God's correction is just that - making sure we get to where we are supposed to be in Him without crash landing or smashing up against a rock wall. God's correction helps us become disciplined in righteousness.

A happy man is the man who finds God's wisdom and understanding for his life. Prov. 3:13 **Happy is the man that finds wisdom, and the man that gets understanding.** There is such happiness when a person gets God's wisdom and answer through prayer for a problem that seemed unsolvable. The assurance that wells up in our heart is pure joy when God gives us direction, because we had asked for His wisdom and understanding. James 1:5 **If you need wisdom, ask our generous God, and he will give it to you. He will not rebuke you for asking.**

True happiness comes from the instructions God gives us to be in relationship with Him. The accumulation of stuff will sometimes bring temporary happiness, but will wear out as the same products we once wished for will be replaced by newer and improved ones as they come along.

The happiness that God gives us, through faith in Him, will never wear thin because it is full of God's anointed presence. The Lord's presence in our lives is His gift that gives us true happiness in life. Where the Lord is, there is joy and freedom to be happy. 2Cor. 3:17 **Now the Lord is the Spirit, and where the Spirit of the Lord is, there is freedom.** Happy is the man who receives what God gives him for a righteous life. Happy is that man.

CAN'T GET NO SATISFACTION

Proverbs 30:2 Surely I am only a brute, not a man; I do not have human understanding.

I can't get no satisfaction!

The British rock star and philosopher Mick Jagger has been howling this statement for decades. For many listeners of this old song, the truth of it has come home and has become poignant to the point of heartbreak. Many have traded sex for affection, drugs for enlightenment, and alcohol for strength and courage: all in search of fulfillment. People have traded their values and morals for money.

Many have even exchanged their personal identity for the acceptance of others, resulting in false friendships that come from that exchange. Through it all, they have found no satisfaction for their souls whatsoever. Perhaps we have to ask ourselves the question found in the word of God. Luke 24:5b **Why do you look for the living among the dead?**

Why do we continually keep looking for

purpose and fulfillment in a fallen and destructive environment? Someone might answer, "It is because we live on this earth and are human; therefore, look for satisfaction within the realm of our existence." This answer seems to be right until we come to the fact that we are first a spirit, with a soul, living in a body.

Our first position and existence is spirit. Until the needs of the spirit are met, the rest of our being will be found wanting. 1John 5:7 **For there are three that bear record in heaven, the Father, the Word, and the Holy Ghost: and these three are one.** 8 **And there are three that bear witness in earth, the Spirit, and the water, and the blood: and these three agree in one.**

Satisfaction, contentment, fulfillment, and rest are not commodities that can be bought or exchanged on an open-market as advertised twenty-four-seven by the many media outlets in this world. Paul the Apostle said that he had learned to become content. Phil. 4:11 **I am not saying this because I am in need, for I have learned to be content whatever the circumstances.**

Contentment, satisfaction, and fulfillment are

disciplines and acquired skills that we grow into by the leading of the Holy Spirit. Happiness is often circumstantial, but satisfaction is a state of being. True enough, I can't get no satisfaction in this world system; however, I can get it in the kingdom of God. Matt. 11:28 **Come to me, all you who are weary and burdened, and I will give you rest.**

So how I do change the tune of that old song in my life? How do I get satisfaction in this life? A very good instruction given to us by the Apostle Paul is stated in Gal. 5:16 **This I say then, "Walk in the Spirit, and ye shall not fulfill the lust of the flesh."** First things first. Walk, react, talk, and go forward in the spirit of God who lives in you and is leading you through your conscience to do what the Lord has already instructed you to do through His word.

If we do this we will not fall to the seductions of all the sins that are available to each one of us. When we start to focus on living by putting the spirit first then satisfaction, contentment, fulfillment, and peace will come up to the forefront of our beings. Some will say to me at this point, "I do not read the bible as much as I should. How do I get to the point of the Apostle Paul's instruction?" This is the dilemma going on in the body of Christ today.

People want all the blessings of God without growing in a relationship with Him. A worldly saying that describes this problem would be "Everyone wants to park in the shade, but no one wants to plant a tree." God has made it possible for every person on this earth, regardless of race, nation, language, status, or anything else that designates a human being, to come to Him and have a relationship. Growth in that relationship comes through His word. Rom. 10:17 **So then faith comes by hearing, and hearing by the word of God.**

I am not advocating a bunch of "Thou shall do and thou shall not do" to get true satisfaction in our lives. I am saying that authentic satisfaction comes from a relationship with God and is developed and nurtured just as much and even more than with spouse or friends. Become satisfied in God and who He is in your life, then you will become satisfied with who you are. Become satisfied in the Lord and you will become satisfied in your own skin.

Satisfaction is found in the kingdom of God, not the realms of this temporal world system. Yes, we all live in this world, but put God first and the world system will not live in you. Matt. 6:33 **But seek first his kingdom and his righteousness, and all these things will be given to you as well.**

THAT THING CALLED MORE

Proverbs 11:25 Give freely and become more wealthy; be stingy and lose everything.

The Consumer they call us. We're the people that buy. Quote from Canadian singer Stompin' Tom Connors.

Retail therapy is a therapy many live and set their lives to. There is such a drive in our society to want more and the leaders of our consumerist system make it easy to get more and more of all that can be thought of. More of what you might ask? Just more, that is what many seem to want - more. More money, more house, more boat or car, more food, more vacation, and more of more.

We have become melancholic looking for home in this rapid lifestyle of acquiring more of anything imaginable. The anxiousness that is deep down inside the everyday person cannot be explained away; it gnaws at the center of our being. Most people know there is more to life than owning stuff, but they no longer know how to divorce themselves from all the stuff that is thought to be needed.

There seems to be a pressure on Christian people of whom many want to be secure in the love of God, but the system we live in won't let us be secure unless we buy our way out. Life is spiritually discerned and we need to know what the Holy Spirit says about going forward in life.

God knew we would be wrestling this thing called more, because He created us to want more. We were created to want more of God. The Lord put a desire in us to want more of the power of the Holy Spirit. We have been inspired by God to want more relationship with Christ our savior, but the enemy of our soul has diverted our attention to using our wants for more toward the things of the earth with no lasting value.

The devil knows if we are buying stuff all the time, we can become stingy. As the proverb says, "Lose everything." Matt. 6:19 **Do not store up for yourselves treasures on earth, where moths and vermin destroy, and where thieves break in and steal.** Yes, we do need to live here on this earth and we do need to pay our way through life, but not at the cost of being owned by all the possessions we own. We do live in the everyday world where the cost of living is outrageous, in some cases, and God knows this fact.

Solomon, who was the richest man alive, even said that money handles most problems. Eccl. 10:19 **Bread is made for laughter, and wine gladdens life, and money answers everything.** However, as Solomon found out, money itself did not handle the issue of our eternal soul but only worked in earthly matters. The Lord has said clearly to those who follow Him that we make sure we put Christ's kingdom first and the things in this life will get taken care of in this world. Matt. 6:33 **But seek ye first the kingdom of God, and his righteousness; and all these things shall be added unto you.** God also said in Psalm 37:25 **I have been young, and now am old, yet I have not seen the righteous forsaken or his children begging for bread.**

God does want to promote us in this world. The Lord is pleased to give us good things within the realm of His kingdom to help this world. Luke 12:32 **Do not be afraid, little flock, for your Father has been pleased to give you the kingdom.** Our heavenly Father finds delight in giving us our heart's desire. Psalm 21:2 **Thou hast given him his heart's desire, and hast not withheld the request of his lips. Selah.** God shows us when we take a delightful love toward God, He will give us the desires of our heart. Psalm 37:4 **Take delight in the LORD, and he will give you the desires of your heart.**

Retail therapy, or consuming vast amounts of items for the sake of doing something to pass the time, has lost a lot of its shine for many. We were created to be givers and be a blessing in this world by being a hand extended on God's behalf. God is not stingy, yet He has everything. Psalm 24:1 **The earth is the LORD's, and everything in it. The world and all its people belong to him.**

We were created to want more of God so that we can give more of ourselves with God in us. We are enlarging the capacity of our souls when we become more of who God made us to be. When life is over, the stuff we have will only be worth what it can be sold for in a garage sale. What we are made of in heart will follow us into eternity where there will be so much more of life beyond our understanding.

What more do you want than the gift of eternal life with God Himself? If you have Jesus Christ as your Lord, then you have everything and all the things needed to live here will come your way. What an amazing God we serve. Give us more of you, Lord God. Amen!

LIFE OR LIFESTYLE?

Proverbs 14:22 The fear of the LORD is a fountain of life, to depart from the snares of death.

Living or existing? This is a good question. Modern medicine has allowed many people to live longer, but not necessarily giving the person quality of life. Sometimes these individuals end up simply existing and becoming discouraged because they thought the treatment would bring them life. Like any pill or prescription, it does have limitations. People who are looking for the one-hit wonder can become disheartened.

Living is a choice, not just a thing absorbed through osmosis because it is around us. Living must be acted upon and lived out of one's soul and being. Deut. 30:19 **This day I call the heavens and the earth as witnesses against you that I have set before you life and death, blessings and curses. Now choose life, so that you and your children may live.**

Another good question is "Are you just looking for lifestyle or life?" We are bombarded with lifestyle ads and television channels pushing lifestyle to the point of excess. Every home and garden show has people looking for lifestyle to the point of neurotic breakdowns if granite countertops are not in the deal. There is nothing wrong with a good, nice, and even extravagant lifestyle, but it should not come at the cost of actually living in the presence of God.

Jesus said that He was the life. He did not say He was a lifestyle to build one's personal agenda or belief system around. John 14:6 **Jesus answered, "I am the way and the truth and the life. No one comes to the Father except through me."** The same thing goes for choosing life, rather than just existing. The Lord said that He had come to give us life and abundant life at that. John 10:10b **I am come that they might have life, and that they might have it more abundantly.**

The Scribes and Pharisees had turned the laws and oracles of God into a lifestyle, rather than an opportunity for a relational life with God. As God said on different occasions, the people were not for Him in their hearts but only in what they could get out of Him. Isa. 29:13 **The Lord says, "These people come near to me with**

their mouth and honor me with their lips, but their hearts are far from me. Their worship of me is based on merely human rules they have been taught." Existing in a religious lifestyle had become more important than a life in God.

Jesus was encountering the same thing with the Scribes and Pharisees. They were choosing a religious lifestyle of many man-made ordinances in order to earn the love and affirmation of God in their lives. At the same time, they questioned any other lifestyle outside of their own, even if God was making the argument for life. Matt. 15:2 **Why do your disciples disobey our age-old tradition? For they ignore our tradition of ceremonial hand washing before they eat.**

Jesus had a way of disrupting the traditional lifestyle the Pharisees and Scribes had invented through the arduous implementation of the laws. Jesus, with righteousness and the life of God, changed the way things were seen by properly interpreting the same laws. Matt. 15:3 **Jesus replied, "And why do you break the command of God for the sake of your tradition?"** In this same bible chapter, Jesus goes on to point out the laws of God are corrupted for the sake of their own lifestyle.

Have you found yourself in a position of an argument with God over lifestyle, rather than life He has declared? If you are insisting on a particular lifestyle and it is causing a corrosiveness in the relationship between you and God, then it might be time to give it up. What on earth is worth the damage of your soul?

In the book of Ecclesiastes, Solomon spends a monetary fortune looking through every type of lifestyle imaginable for the answers of eternal life. He knows there is a need for a rebirth, so to speak, but cannot find it in anything under the sun. He comes to the conclusion that under the sun all is vanity, but the answer is in what God says. Eccl. 12:13 **Now all has been heard; here is the conclusion of the matter: Fear God and keep his commandments, for this is the duty of all mankind.** 14 **For God will bring every deed into judgment, including every hidden thing, whether it is good or evil.**

What does Solomon conclude? Chose a life with and in the Lord rather than the lifestyles offered by the world system with no real answers. Chose life, because Jesus is the life. Amen!

THINGS WANT TO GROW

Proverbs 12:14 A man shall be satisfied with good by the fruit of his mouth: and the hard work of a man's hands shall be rendered unto him.

I was talking with my good friend, Tim, who is a horticulturist and landscape architect extraordinaire. I showed him a grafting project I was working on; an old grape vine in my yard. I had cut down the four-inch thick vine to about a foot and a half off the ground and established some notch grafts that I grafted into the old vine.

There were problems with the old variety and the choice was to take it right out and plant a new kind of vine, or try this notch graft method. I am grafting three different varieties of grapes into this one old established grapevine.

One of the graft buds had opened and looked good and healthy. With emphasis and a knowing look on his face, Tim said, "Things want to grow." The truth of that statement hit my heart with profound clarity. Everything God makes wants to grow. The entire earth system is designed to want to grow.

As we looked at the new graft that had strongly taken, we could see the workings of the word of God in the healthy graft. Jesus said in John 15:5 **"I am the vine; you are the branches. If you remain in me and I in you, you will bear much fruit; apart from me you can do nothing."** What is so heartwarming to me is that I am grafting a white table grape called a Himrod and a dark purple called a Concord, plus a burnish red called Valiant into this old vine. Think about it. Three different varieties living from one main vine.

The parallels are so wonderful, as each one of us who are in Christ has been grafted into Jesus the true vine. Those of us in Christ are individual branches bringing forth fruit that is characteristic to our individuality that God created within each one of us. However, even though we are individuals, we are one in Christ because we are grafted and fed by Christ's love, truth, and power making us who we are in the body of the Lord.

Jesus really is the vine and we are the branches that bear fruit for His glory and kingdom. It just makes me want to smile and say, "I love you, Lord God. You are so good and you absolutely know what you are doing in this world and in our lives."

Things want to grow. God has put a desire and a purpose within each one of us, as we grow, to produce Godly fruit in life. God, the vine keeper, comes along and prunes what does not produce fruit. John 15:2 **He cuts off every branch in me that bears no fruit, while every branch that does bear fruit he prunes so that it will be even more fruitful.** God's purpose for us is that we produce more and more of what is Godly.

We are pruned in order to keep producing much more fruit as we grow, plus we are to become a healthy branch that can be counted on to nourish the weak and grow into what God has created us to be. John 15:8 **This is to my Father's glory, that you bear much fruit, showing yourselves to be my disciples.**

It is the will of God that we grow up, grow outward, and grow strong in the richness of the fruit of the Holy Spirit. Gal. 5:22 **But the fruit of the Spirit is love, joy, peace, longsuffering, gentleness, goodness, faith,** 23 **meekness, temperance: against such there is no law.**

Within each one of us is the God-given ability to be grafted into Christ and become one with the Father as Jesus is one with the Father. John 17:21 **I pray that they will all be one, just as you and I are one-as you are in me, Father, and I am in you. And may they be in us so that the world will believe you sent me.**

As I have been working in the garden and cultivating around the vines, fruit trees, and berry bushes this year, I have often stated out loud what my friend Tim said, "Things want to grow." It feels like I am making a declaration of faith when I speak it out.

I become aware that Christ is working a work within me that spurs me onward to the heavenly calling God has put within me. Jude 1:24 **Now to him who is able to keep you from stumbling and to present you blameless before the presence of his glory with great joy.** May we all come to the place where we welcome the pruning the Father does in our lives so that we can grow mightily in Christ. Blessings on us all.

PART TWO:

QUESTIONS FOR UNDERSTANDING

1. *What did you learn in this section of the book?*
2. *What surprised you the most?*
3. *What subject(s) spoke to your heart?*
4. *Did the material that you read help you understand the subject(s) more or less?*
5. *What topics are important to you? Why?*
6. *How do these articles relate to you?*
7. *After reading this section of the book, what will you change in your life?*

PART THREE:

BATTLING FALSEHOOD

1 Kings 18:21

Then Elijah approached all the people and said, "How long will you waver between two opinions? If the LORD is God, follow him. But if Baal, follow him." But the people didn't answer him a word.

FROO FROO PHILOSOPHY

Proverbs 18:24 A man who has friends must himself be friendly, but there is a friend who sticks closer than a brother.

Jami Rogers said, "Never dismiss someone's experience or feelings by trying to make your situation or someone else's situation seem so much worse. That is called emotional dismissiveness."

I feel I am going to bat for my friend Jami. She and many others struggle with false and empty friendships, beliefs, and relationships that lead nowhere but to loneliness and emotional hurts. Hag.1:9a **You expected much, but then it amounted to little.**

The myriads of "philosophical how to get along books" often do not have the essential ingredients for honest friendships. These books have a lot of tactical advice for becoming popular and standing out in the crowd, but not the clear and sincere directions needed for being who you are when your guard is down, or risking who you are when you put your heart out there in open view of the masses.

Some of our human needs are to be loved, heard, valued, and accepted. However, finding fulfillment for these needs in a broken world may not be realistic without first knowing with certainty the Lord's love for us personally. Jer. 1:5a **I chose you before I formed you in the womb; I set you apart before you were born.**

Knowing God's love for us is our pivotal heart's position to launch from in any other relationship. If we do not trust the love of God for ourselves personally, then trusting those who are in this fallen world will be a difficult and a continuous workload of striving.

Philosophy alone cannot meet the deepest heartfelt need of existence. This is why we sometimes one-up the other person with an emotional dismissive attitude, because our own emotions in life are lacking assurance. Only God Himself can fill that empty space in our hearts, because He created us to need His presence within our souls so we could be fully who we are. Phil. 2:13 **For it is God who works in you to will and to act on behalf of His good pleasure.**

We were created to know in our hearts that

when we call on God's name we are clearly heard by Him. Jer. 33:3 **Call to me, and I will answer you; I will tell you wonderful and marvelous things that you know nothing about.** Because I know the Lord has already accepted me through Jesus Christ, I am willing by faith to risk being friendly as the proverb says. Prov. 18:24a **A man who has friends must himself be friendly.**

Our acceptance has already been established within our Creator's love; therefore, being accepted by our friends and those we come across in our daily lives will become easier, because the sour smell of personal uncertainty is not emanating from our being.

By the power of the Holy Spirit, we have a humble confidence within Christ that philosophy cannot generate. When we know we are the beloved in Christ and are at peace within ourselves, we will be able to be friendly in this hard world.

Christ has given us His ability to be that person who sticks closer than a brother. Froo froo and pseudo-philosophy can only show us an insipid idea, path, or repetitive rote activity to help curtail certain unwanted habits. Col. 2:8 **Beware lest any man spoil you through philosophy and vain**

deceit, after the tradition of men, after the rudiments of the world, and not after Christ.

This froo froo or vain philosophy is a temporary patch on the tattered fabric of lost and hurt souls. A real life change is needed. Jesus, who is the way, the truth, and the life can change our hearts and lives to become His accepted righteousness forever and ever. I'll take what the Lord has done for me any day. Thank you, Lord God.

SLASH AND BURN

Proverbs 29:8 Scoffers set a city in a flame; But wise men turn away wrath.

Slash and burn is a term used to describe farming methods. However, when used to describe a strong person's attitude toward a life choice it means extremely ruthless, unsparing, aggressive, and merciless. Christians should have this attitude when it comes to destroying the works of the devil. A slash and burn policy that is ruthless and aggressive should be one of our raison d'être when fighting the wicked works perpetrated by the enemy of our soul.

When we fight the good fight of faith, we are to be as cunning as serpents and as gentle as doves while not giving any place for the devil to rule anywhere in our lives. Eph. 4:27 **Do not give the devil an opportunity.** James 4:7 **Submit yourselves therefore to God. Resist the devil, and he will flee from you.**

If we do not submit to God's way of fighting the good fight of faith, we can find ourselves simply quoting scripture without faith. The result of this slackness of heart can backfire and we simply become sloganeers of Christian jargon and not doers of God's word. James 1:22 **But be ye doers of the word, and not hearers only, deceiving your own selves.**

The thought of slash and burn policies always leaves us with visions of large swaths of the jungle or forested areas seen through a smokey film of charred stumps to make room for industrial use. We see miles and miles of scarred landscape in the middle of pristine country. Let us reverse the process by walking through large swaths of stolen territory that Satan took and transform it back into God's paradise.

If we were unsparing and merciless when it came to destroying the works of the devil through prayer and being a hand extended from God, we would have great victories in Christ. We could help the next generation fulfill their call and purpose in life.

Each generation has something to offer mankind. We were created with a purpose, and on purpose, by the will of God to bring life to this lost and fractured world. 2Cor. 5:18 **And all**

things are of God, who hath reconciled us to himself by Jesus Christ, and hath given to us the ministry of reconciliation; 19 **that is, in Christ God was reconciling the world to himself, not counting their trespasses against them, and entrusting to us the message of reconciliation.**

We were created to bring and restore friendship with God through God's plan of salvation and direction. Each one of us has a part of the puzzle that can help mend the ripped relationship that divides many people from God and each other.

We need the diversity God created within mankind to bring out the whole plan God has for His world. The devil tries to corrupt our hearts by deceiving us into thinking that all humanity under God is impossible. Satan wants us bigoted and ethnically divided. He knows, united under God, we are the most powerful force on earth.

United in the Lord can burn and expose the destructive lies of the enemy. Lev. 26:8 **Five of you shall chase a hundred, and a hundred of you shall put ten thousand to flight: and your enemies shall fall before you by the sword.** With God leading us, we can put the devil to flight and keep him running.

People who make end of life statements or deathbed confessions never proclaim "I should have spent more time at work, or I should have ripped off more people." A statement like "I should have owned more stuff" would sound like nonsense at the time of departure from this world. The things that come to heart and mind as we get older are deep soul issues. Things that are weighty and of eternal value have more importance to our souls.

We question our own hearts as to whether we fulfilled our life purpose and calling. Were we part of the problem, or were we the force God made us to be in this earth through Christ the Lord? As for me, it is time to take on a slash and burn attitude through Christ over sin and deception. Let us rise up and slash the devil's plans and burn his lies by entering into a closer relationship with our Lord and Savior Jesus Christ. Amen and amen!

OFFENDED WITH THE OFFENDED

Proverbs 18:19 An offended friend is harder to win back than a fortified city. Arguments separate friends like a gate locked with bars.

John Bevere said, "An offended heart is the breeding ground of deception."

Being offended in most cases is a personal choice. I choose to be offended at what my wife, friend, boss, or an authority in life said to me. How have we become such an offended society that we are so easily offended at other's offences? It has turned to the ridiculous when we hear someone say, "I'm offended that they are offended." Really? Have we become such a touchy-feely people that the first reaction to any slight is offendedness?

I recently had the opportunity to be offended when my book cover posters were rejected, because someone had been offended by them hanging on display in a bookstore. I was about to become offended at the offended when I realized it was just a matter of taste in design and art. It had not been myself personally who had been rejected; therefore, there was no need to enter into the offence. I was not going to be the reason that friends separated because of a perceived offence. Prov. 18:19 **An offended friend is harder to win back than a fortified city. Arguments separate friends like a gate locked with bars.**

This whole event got me thinking on how thin-skinned we have become and how sensitive we are to being snubbed or criticized, even if it is constructive criticism. I almost fell for the self-deception of becoming offended for nothing and would have become a stumbling block to someone taking sides in the offence. Have we become our own stumbling block? Luke 17:1 **Jesus said to His disciples, "It is inevitable that stumbling blocks will come, but woe to the one through whom they come!"**

Jesus said to pray for those who cause us problems in life and not to murder them with our words and attitudes. The Lord says that offences will come, but to take the high road when dealing with an offence. Matt. 11:6 **And blessed is he who is not offended because of Me.**

We read in the book of Genesis what can happen when an offence takes root and turns to raw anger. Cain killed his brother over the fact that Abel brought an acceptable sacrifice to God. Cain's offendedness at God turned to murderous hatred for his brother. Joseph's brothers betrayed Joseph and sold him into slavery because they were offended at the love Jacob had for his son. Their offence turned to a murderous plot of revenge and eventually they settled for selling him for a profit. The offences of these people turned to self-deception and allowed them to rationalize their evil actions.

History shows us that a slight or offence taken too far can result in wars and entire people groups eradicated through ethnic cleansing. People choose to be offended, but the choice is also ours to not pick up the offence and personalize it to the point of madness.

Our counseling office sessions are full of married couples who have allowed offences to fester and become gangrenous to their relationships. The love they once had for each other has turned to a score-keeping record of who hurt who the most. I'm not saying that some marriages do not have real problems, but so many of the problems could have been settled with the words "I'm sorry I hurt you. Please forgive me."

The Lord warned us that persecution, unjust accusations, and outright slander would be a result of accepting Jesus as Lord. John 16:1 **These things have I spoken unto you, that ye should not be offended.** Jesus also remarked that others would be offended because we had accepted Jesus as our personal Savior. However, the Lord has given us the ability to overcome all this through His love and power, but we have to make the choice to do so.

Saints, offences will come and the opportunity to pick them up will also come. Let us try and create a not-offended free zone in our hearts and lives. Let us position ourselves in a place where we do not pick up an offence, but rather choose peace in Him who first loved us with real love. Amen!

E STANDS FOR EVIDENCE

Proverbs 6:2 You have been trapped by what you said, ensnared by the words of your mouth.

The way I see it, the e in email stands for evidence. This week in the news another politician had to resign because of embarrassing photos and explicit emails. More frat boys were expelled because of questionable behavior. That behavior was posted online and emailed around. An executive of a company is being called out because of old email posts that expressed her negative views on a minority group of people. She is now having to answer for it. Num. 32:23 **But if you fail to keep your word, then you will have sinned against the LORD, and you may be sure that your sin will find you out.** Haven't people figured out yet that everything that is written in an email and sent is forever in the world system and can be retrieved at any time?

What makes people think they can get away with bragging about secrets in their lives when it is plastered all over the world by their friends, coworkers, and family? The old Benjamin Franklin saying, "Three can keep a secret, if two of them are dead" is apropos to heed in this tell-all tabloid world.

If you have a secret and want it kept, then tell absolutely no one. But whatever you do, don't post it on the world-wide-web. Eccl. 10:20 **Never make light of the king, even in your thoughts. And don't make fun of the powerful, even in your own bedroom. For a little bird might deliver your message and tell them what you said.** I reckon the little bird, in this case, would be Twitter.

It is wisdom to keep our slanders and false accusations to ourselves, because if we spread lies and half-truths all over the place we will be judged for it. Matt. 12:36 **I tell you that on the day of judgment people will have to account for every careless word they speak.** In the same way that we should think before we hit the send button on an email, we should also think before we hit the send button of our mouth. Will the words I am about to say give life or a bruised lashing to someone's soul? Is what I am saying uplifting, or just more negative rhetoric?

We can become as careless as these people who post their idiocy online and not think about the consequences.

What we say matters. It shows us and our fellow man who we really are. Luke 6:45 **A good man out of the good treasure of his heart brings forth good; and an evil man out of the evil treasure of his heart brings forth evil. For out of the abundance of the heart his mouth speaks.** Our mouth will eventually say what is in our heart. This is why we need a new regenerated heart created by the Lord and the finished work of the cross.

It is Christ within us, changing us day-by-day to live and move in the power of the Holy Spirit. Would Jesus be posting slanders and the nastiest words online? Of course not. Then why are some who claim to walk with Christ posting cruelties and plotting vengeful thoughts? James 3:10 **And so blessing and cursing come pouring out of the same mouth. Surely, my brothers and sisters, this is not right!**

If you want to change your words, then change your focus. Phil. 4:8 **Finally, brethren, whatsoever things are true, whatsoever**

things are honest, whatsoever things are just, whatsoever things are pure, whatsoever things are lovely, whatsoever things are of good report; if there be any virtue, and if there be any praise, think on these things. Start hanging around people who still believe in honor and forthrightness of character for life. Stop the gossip in its tracks.

Before you decide to post something you are not sure of and whether it should even be posted in the first place, remember the e in email may come back to visit you. Col. 3:23 Whatever you do, do it from the heart, as something done for the Lord and not for people. Amen and amen!

BETWIXT AND BETWEEN

Proverbs 1:29 For that they hated knowledge, and did not choose the fear of the LORD.

1Kings 18:21 **Elijah stood in front of them and said, "How much longer will you try to have things both ways? If the LORD is God, worship him! But if Baal is God, worship him!" The people did not say a word.**

Having it both ways seems to be the desired way of life that people from the past wanted life to be. If we take stock of our own lives today, it seems things have not changed. Wanting both good and bad all the time with no consequences or accountability seems to be the goal of government and special interest groups.

Give me gluttony and greed with no effect to my body or personality. Give me envy and lust with no stain on my character. Allow me to reign my life with pride and wrath with no consequences or responsibility for any of my actions. When we take on this secular default setting we do not become a tolerant society, we become a nation of sloths with no ability to make righteous choices in life. We become susceptible to any kind of nonsense offered to our souls.

God asks us to make a personal and solid choice because lukewarmness - the state of many people today - will keep them in a place of non-effectiveness and with no authoritative power to move forward in life. Rev. 3:16 **So, because you are lukewarm, and neither hot nor cold, I am going to vomit you out of my mouth.**

When we are hot or cold God can do something with us, because we have made a solid decision. However, lukewarmness - an insipid emotional state, or a lack of enthusiasm in life - makes it hard for God or anyone to help humanity make a qualitative life decision with the forthrightness of heart. People are stuck between two opinions; therefore, going nowhere fast.

This view of life is all around us and makes it hard for the general population to get a grip on what to do. The government subsidizes big agriculture to produce products for junk food and promotes the overuse of chemicals and poisoning fertilizers, while at the same time telling us to eat more vegetables and make healthier choices.

The governing financial leaders create easy credit of all kinds persuading people into ever-increasing and higher amounts of debt, while expressing concern about the debt and suggesting restraint and control in order to keep paying the never-ending debt. They want it both ways and expect a sane decision from the population they are manipulating.

The credit score is a common phrase among our youth, rather than the idea of earning and saving up for a particular item. Duplicity and subterfuge is the norm that comes out of our institutions, and confusion with the lack of ability to make a hot or cold decision is the result. Many students come out of college and university bewildered and believing in nothing because of the non-ethical view taught on morality and keeping a clean conscience, thus creating a new generation of sloths who are stuck betwixt and between the ability to make sound judgments.

I do believe there are some good instructors, politicians, and advisers who are truly trying to make a difference for the betterment of our lives and country. However, they seem to be voices in the wilderness. Their numbers may be few, but thank God they are there. This is why we, as individual people, have to step up to the plate of life and make positive and righteous choices in our lives. This way we will not be dependent on the governing institutions to make our decisions for us.

If the will of the people is the will of a righteous and loving God, then God will do His part in changing the hearts of the leaders and kings of industry to reflect a desired blessed and healthy life. Prov. 21:1 **The king's heart is like a stream of water directed by the LORD; he guides it wherever he pleases.**

When we, as individuals, clean up our own backyard and take the Lord at His word, we will make sound choices that are conducive to the health and blessing of one another and our nation. Hopefully then, over time, common sense may become commonplace. We will grow up and stop being children with no direction stuck betwixt and between something that should be an obvious choice. Eph. 4:14 **Then we will no longer be little children, tossed by the waves and blown around by every wind of teaching, by human cunning with cleverness in the**

techniques of deceit.

Choosing the fear of the Lord or righteousness in Christ with a heart led by integrity should not be odd or a foreign concept to us unless you are - as the Psalmist says - a fool who says there is no God. Psalm 14:1a **The fool hath said in his heart, There is no God.** To remain in a place of no decision is a decision.

If we are not sure how to proceed, we can ask God for His wisdom and He will give it to us. James 1:5 **Now if any of you lacks wisdom, he should ask God—who gives to all generously and ungrudgingly—and it will be given to him.** So we come to the same place Elijah was at when he presented his declaration of choice. Hopefully, we will answer and not stand there not saying a word. I choose the fear of the Lord and His love. Blessings.

TEMPTATIONS COME IN THREES

Proverbs 28:21 It isn't right to be unfair, but some people can be bribed with only a piece of bread.

CS Lewis said, "No man knows how bad he is till he has tried so hard to be good."

The human condition is tempted in three areas of life, just as it always has been and always will be. Man is made up of spirit, soul, and body and all aspects of our human being will be tested.

Jesus was tempted in the desert forty days in the same three areas of life that every individual on earth is tempted in. After fasting forty days the Gospel of Matthew says that Jesus hungered and the devil's temptation was to feed the needs of the flesh. Matt. 4:3 **The tempter came to him and said, "If you are the Son of God, tell these stones to become bread."**

What are your fleshly hungers or cravings that are out of control? Can you be bribed out of your relationship with the Lord with covetous wants? Do you crave your neighbour's house, spouse, car, pay-cheque, or anything else they have? The bread we hunger for can cause us to sin, but like the Lord Jesus, we have the solution - the word of God causes us to triumph. Matt. 4:4 **Jesus answered, "It is written: 'Man shall not live on bread alone, but on every word that comes from the mouth of God.'"**

We will be tempted in the area of our spiritual needs, just as Jesus was. Matt. 4:5 **Then the devil took him to the holy city and had him stand on the highest point of the temple.** It is interesting that the devil tempted Jesus from a position of religious belief. Satan was saying, "Stand on the peak of your religious belief and throw yourself off the ledge in full presumption out of religious fervor. Use your organized religion as your foundation for eternal decisions." Again, Jesus answered the enemy with the word of God. Matt. 4:7 **Jesus answered him, "It is also written: 'Do not put the Lord your God to the test.'"**

Are you being tempted to stand on the soap-box of your religious beliefs to belittle or persecute a sector of the human population that Jesus also died for? Have we become so hell-bent on being right and slandering without grace, based on our denominational platforms?

Jesus asked us to go into the world and preach the good news that His salvation is available to everyone who received it by faith. He did not ask us to point out people's sins or transgressions. That is the Holy Spirit's job. John 16:8 **And when He comes, He will convict the world in regard to sin and righteousness and judgment.**

The temptations that come for the soul is a hard battleground because our emotions are so tangled up in feelings of pride, jealousy, and grandeur. However, we can take heart in the fact that Jesus also overcame this temptation with the word of God; therefore, we have the power to do the same through Christ our Lord.

Matt. 4:8 **Again, the devil took him to a very high mountain and showed him all the kingdoms of the world and their splendor.**
9 **"All this I will give you," he said, "if you will bow down and worship me."** I love the dismissiveness and authority of Jesus' words. Matt. 4:10 **Jesus said to him, "Away from me, Satan! For it is written: 'Worship the Lord your God, and serve him only.'"** No big windup of

indignant speech, just the powerful words "Away from me, Satan!"

When we are tempted to trade in the values of our soul for a morsel of fleeting fame or temporary glory, let us remember that we have a more sure thing than what Satan can offer. The glitz and glam that sparkles for a short time will fizzle out on our deathbeds. Selling our souls for the so-called fifteen minutes of fame is not worth a lost eternity of joy and peace we have in Christ. We have been given the righteous position of being with our heavenly Father, now and forevermore.

Temptations may come in threes, but the power of the Godhead helps us overcome in threes as well. 1John 5:7 **For there are three that bear record in heaven, the Father, the Word, and the Holy Ghost: and these three are one.** God and I are a majority, just as anyone who is in Christ is. We do not need the offers that come from hell to be a somebody. We already are the sons of God. We are the Lord's kings and priests ministering to God. We have a place in life, and it is a beautiful place to be. Thank you, Jesus, for showing us that we too can say, "Satan, In Jesus name, away from me."

DIRTY TRICKS

Proverbs 16:30 With narrowed eyes, people plot evil; with a smirk, they plan their mischief.

Matthew 13:25 **But while everyone was sleeping, his enemy came and sowed weeds among the wheat, and went away.**

I was working with some new grape vines I had planted from containers last year and noticed how well they were doing. They had so many grape clusters on them for just being a few years old, and the weight per cluster was good. Some of the grapes were starting to change toward their color of dark blue. I took a few of the grapes and squeezed them to see the juice content. To my surprise, along with the juice, some seeds came forth as well. "What?" I said in a loud voice. "These are supposed to be seedless grapes! I was told emphatically they were seedless. Who mislabeled these tags identifying this type of grape?" I felt gypped, ripped off, and lost for words because I was sure they were seedless.

I could remedy the situation by creating notch

grafts next spring from other seedless grape buds, but all the extra work and time was bugging me. I thought someone has mislabeled the vines at the nursery and they were actually getting paid a wage to make these errors. Matt. 7:16 **You can identify them by their fruit, that is, by the way they act. Can you pick grapes from thorn bushes, or figs from thistles?** Where was the pride of doing a good job? Col. 3:23 **Whatever you do, work at it with all your heart, as working for the Lord, not for human masters.** I was just venting loud thoughts throughout my mind and scripture was flowing at rapid speed. "Settle down," I said to myself. "It's only a couple of vines and this can be fixed."

I went to the plant nursery with sample grape clusters, the tags with the type and seedless label, plus the receipt. I presented all the information to the head-gardener. All she could do was give me some new seedless grapevines as compensation and replacement. She was sorry, but the error had been done at their supplier and not at their facility.

While I was there I noticed they had some of the same grapes with the same labels, so we went over to them and a few of them had some small clusters. She checked them. Sure enough, the grapes had seeds and were also mislabeled. She said, "We will most likely be getting a lot of calls in the near future because of this mess-up." I empathised for her. I realized that for me the mix up will be a bit more work to get the type of grapes growing I want, but for the head-gardener, it will be a customer relations mess. Whether this was done by accident or on purpose, this turned out to be a dirty trick on a lot of people.

What an object lesson this was turning out to be. I thought of what the gospel of Matthew says. Matt. 13:25 **But while everyone was sleeping, his enemy came and sowed weeds among the wheat, and went away.** This is what the enemy of our soul does on a regular basis. The devil's number one agenda is plotting and sowing dirty tricks into our lives to destroy those who are in Christ. As the scripture implies, he comes under the cloak of darkness and sows his seeds of doubt, mistrust, and anger into the soil of our hearts to disrupt the wonderful work of the new birth Christ has done in us through the cross and His blood.

The devil uses people who pretend to walk

with God to sow seeds of betrayal and hurt into our lives. Phil. 3:18 **For as I have often told you before, and now declare even with tears: Many live as enemies of the cross of Christ.** However, the truth of God's word is we have overcome the world through the work of the cross and our faith in the blood Jesus shed for us.

There are those who will plot evil and smirk with plans of mischief toward the saints of the Lord. They will always have a dirty tricks campaign going on to try and defeat those who are in Christ, but as the Lord says, the weeds will be gathered and burned and the wheat will be gathered for the Lord's use. As for my grape problem, I will transplant the mislabeled grapes along the fence in early spring. As summer comes along, I will enjoy the green beauty of them. Thank you, Lord, for turning this trick around. Amen.

WHO IS RESPONSIBLE?

Proverbs 7:1 My son, keep my words and store up my commands within you.

I have been teaching a class on the responsibility we have as individuals for our spiritual growth as well as our emotional, mental, and physical well-being. We represent the kingdom of God, and we have the Spirit of the Lord within us. Rom. 8:11 **If the Spirit of him who raised Jesus from the dead dwells in you, he who raised Christ Jesus from the dead will also give life to your mortal bodies through his Spirit who dwells in you.**

Why do we have such a hard time living victoriously since the word of God says the resurrection power of God lives in us? It seems we live in a blame-shifting society, and it has become the responsibility of others for our outcome in life. The Twinkie defense has become mainstream and is now leaking into church life. People use frequent excuses like "It is the pastor's fault I am stagnating in my Christian growth. The loud music makes it too hard to praise and worship."

Taking responsibility for our actions is the only way we are going to grow from glory to glory. If we do not take ownership of our actions, then we will always be at the same place, repeating the same old thing that got us the negative result in the first place. We will look for someone or something to blame because the spiritual results in our lives will be hit and miss, with missing most of the time.

We see this blame game happening when God asks Adam if he had eaten from the tree of good and evil. Gen. 3:11b **Hast thou eaten of the tree, whereof I commanded thee that thou should not eat?** Adam blames God personally. He also blames the woman for his own choice of eating the forbidden fruit. Gen. 3:12 **The man replied, "It was the woman you gave me who gave me the fruit, and I ate it."** The woman blames the beguiling serpent. Gen. 3:13 **And the LORD God said unto the woman, "What is this that thou hast done?" And the woman said, "The serpent beguiled me, and I did eat."**

I'm not saying I would have done any differently in Adam's place. What we see is that sin causes us to shift the blame and responsibility of our sin onto others. It seems to be our default nature. However, if we are in Christ we are no longer of that old spirit. We can now come clean because the blood of Jesus washes us from shame and blame.

The Lord invites us to come to Him as quickly as possible when we have made a wrong choice in life. When we sin, God says to come to Him and confess it the moment we realize we have missed the mark. Heb. 4:16 **Therefore we should come with boldness to the throne of grace, so that we may receive mercy and may find grace for help in time of need.** We are invited to 'fess up and take responsibility for what we have done. If we do, God is faithful to forgive us right then and there.1John 1:9 **If we confess our sins, he is faithful and just to forgive us our sins and to cleanse us from all unrighteousness.**

The only way to grow is to admit errors and learn from them. The only way to learn from the mess-ups in life is to take ownership of what we have done, what we are doing, and what we will do in all areas of life. Then we can move forward as mature people of God and become proficient in keeping the words of the Lord stored up within our souls.

Proverbs 7:1 **My son, keep my words and store up my commands within you.** Who is responsible for my life choices? I am responsible. God has given me a free will to choose Him over the insipid fluff the world offers twenty-four-seven. Since we are responsible for what we do in life, let us come boldly to the throne of God and admit our need for His mercy and grace to help us grow in Christ. Blessings.

SERVANT TO THE LENDER

Proverbs 17:18 It's poor judgment to guarantee another person's debt or put up security for a friend.

Debt, debt, and more debt is the spirit at work in this world. We, well meaning parents, are encouraging our children to go into slavery in a roundabout way. Prov. 22:7 **The rich rules over the poor, and the borrower is servant to the lender.** For the sake of a diploma that does not guarantee a good job or career in any of the fields the student is studying through, we have pushed the education mantra on these students to the point of ridiculous debt. Make no mistake: the borrower is a servant to the lender.

Garry Mason, who writes for the Globe And Mail, states in his article *Another Day Smarter, But Deeper In Debt* "To see what can happen when a student debt problem goes unaddressed, one only has to look to the United States, where the situation has reached crisis levels."

The amount of outstanding student debt

there has topped one trillion dollars. That amount, and the delinquencies, are escalating at frightening rates. A Bank of Montreal student survey released last month in April 2014 revealed that postsecondary students expect to graduate from school with more than $26,000 in debt, on average. Students in British Columbia are expected to be nearly $35,000 or more in debt.

Why are parents encouraging their sons and daughters to acquire such debt? Is it because these same parents have learned to be a debt servant to all their own masters and do not know any other way?

One of the conditions for my youngest son to return and live at home so that he could finish his last two years of college for a business degree was that there would be no student loans of any kind. I said if that was the way he wanted to go about getting his education, then there was no point in moving back home because I would be enabling him to believe the lie that so many students have bought into.

I would be helping him become a servant slave to the government and bank lenders of this easy to get money, but oh so hard to pay it back.

My son did not like what I had proposed, but agreed to my terms. He had to work two jobs and do his studies. At the end of the two year study program, he had graduated with a good average and debt free. He was not a servant to anyone or any financial institution. He was able to start his life debt free and not have a financial albatross hanging around his neck like so many other students.

Students have signed up for these unsecured loans and debt in droves. They start life with a huge debt-load before they even have their first career job. The devil is now managing their time, and time for God and ministry will not be affordable on Satan's payment plan.

These gullible students have signed contracts of unsecured loans that are setting a lifestyle precedence in their lives. Debt will become a way of living. Prov. 6:2 **Thou art snared with the words of thy mouth, thou art taken with the words of thy mouth. 5 Deliver thyself as a roe from the hand of the hunter, and as a bird from the hand of the fowler.**

I am often asked for help by the parents of these debt-loaded students who have cornered themselves with an overwhelming amount of debt. Oddly, the parents often want another loan or a guarantor to get themselves and their prodigy out of debt by acquiring more debt. That is the problem. You cannot get out of debt by entering into more debt. They have become a poor risk to others and themselves, but can no longer see it.

This thinking has become a heart and character problem, not a money issue. The feeling that is tearing them apart is the fact that they are servants to the lender. They have become full-time slaves. These slaves to debt are no longer free. They now know it deep down in their hearts, but cannot find a way out. They find it hard to live for Christ. All their time is used up serving another master with great payments. Matt. 6:24 **No man can serve two masters: for either he will hate the one, and love the other; or else he will hold to the one, and despise the other. Ye cannot serve God and mammon.**

We were created to live free in Christ and not put ourselves into bondage of any kind. This method of slow death and drudgery is an attack on the church, because the debt mentality has crept into the church. This is one of the plans of the enemy of our soul.

If Satan can have you working all the time to cover the debt on things you do not need to impress people you do not like, then the devil has got your use of time scheduled for life. Rom. 13:8 **Let no debt remain outstanding, except the continuing debt to love one another, for whoever loves others has fulfilled the law.**

Is saving and working for something of value hard? Sometimes it is, but well worth it when you own it and it does not own you. Over time when the children of the old testament were sold into slavery to cover the accumulated debt because of a chosen lifestyle, there is a moral deficit that comes across the land along with drought, famine, and war. Do we, as a nation, have to go through these events to find out that the borrower is a servant to the lender? I pray not. Hag. 1:5 **Now therefore thus saith the LORD of hosts; Consider your ways.**

ENDEMIC FINGER POINTING

Proverbs 16:3 Commit to the LORD whatever you do, and he will establish your plans.

Everything in life is a result of the choices you made. If you want different results, make different choices.

I was at the doctor's office this week for my yearly physical. One of the things that came up was the great progress I had made with the health of my heart that misses a beat. One of the clinic nurses asked me how I had come so far from the mess I was in four years ago, to the healthy place I am right now. I said, "The first thing I had to do was take full responsibility for damaging my heart and for treating it like third class baggage. I caused the problem with the poor life choices that I had made. If there was going to be a fix, I had to make sure I did not point fingers at anyone but myself. I caused it; therefore, it was up to me to be a major participant in the healing of it."

It would be easy to point my finger at all the processed, nitrate-filled, sugar-packed and GMO products that have become commonplace in our food system. I could point and blame the easy accessibility of drive-thru convenience every time my fat cells screamed for attention. I could make up excuses for shoving all the rubbish down my throat because of the stress I had put myself under.

Then I could keep making up excuses on a regular basis as to why I can't exercise because of the business in my so-called important life. Yup, I could head in that direction of blame and finger pointing. However, the truth would still be that I had willfully made all those choices. The result of those choices was heart disease. Gal. 6:7 **Be not deceived; God is not mocked: for whatsoever a man sows, that shall he also reap.**

I find it interesting that people who made the choice to smoke cigarettes are now pointing their fingers and suing the companies that fulfilled their desire to smoke. People who consume gallons of soft drinks are complaining and pointing fingers at the pop companies for their ailments of obesity and diabetes. Rehab for every imaginable problem is available for people who have become perpetual victims of circumstance, while taking no responsibility whatsoever for their own choices. Endemic finger pointing has become a national pastime.

The first step to recovery of any kind is to admit there is a problem in the first place. Recovery means taking responsibility for the problem you caused in your own life. Admit it, confess it, then you are finally in a position to get rid of it. James 5:16a **Therefore, confess your faults to one another and pray for one another, so that you may be healed.**

I remember when I made the choice to eat real food, only after I had taken responsibility for the poor health I was in. Was it easy? No! Good and real food preparation is really inconvenient, but too bad, it had to be done. I remember the struggle of getting into regular exercise and sticking to it every day. Was it easy? Absolutely not! But too bad, it had to be done. Prov. 16:3 **Commit to the LORD whatever you do, and he will establish your plans.** The finger pointing stops here.

I do not know who or what you have been blaming for all your woes in life, but it has got to stop just for the sake of sanity. In most cases, your boss is not your problem. The teacher is not your child's problem. Your spouse is not your problem. Stop pointing the finger and realize that most likely you are your own problem. Our prayer should be "Lord, fix me."

Take responsibility for the choices you have made. Make new choices to change the course of your life. You will need God's help to do it, and He is right there waiting for you to ask Him for that help. Psalm 46:1 **God is our strong refuge; he is truly our helper in times of trouble.**

I'm not sure why endemic finger pointing has become a default setting in our thinking. But as for me, I have got to constantly look at my own actions to make sure I am walking the walk God put before me. When I stand before God on that great day, I will be standing alone and none of the people or reasons for blame will be there to point at. Since this is the case, I may as well learn to take responsibility now and live in the peace God instructs me to live in through His word now. Time to man-up. Blessings and God's ability be in and on you. Amen.

PART THREE:

QUESTIONS FOR UNDERSTANDING

1. *What did you learn in this section of the book?*
2. *What surprised you the most?*
3. *What subject(s) spoke to your heart?*
4. *Did the material that you read help you understand he subject(s) more or less?*
5. *What topics are important to you? Why?*
6. *How do these articles relate to you?*
7. *After reading this section of the book, what will you change in your life?*

PART FOUR:

STAYING POSITIVE

Being positive in Christ will give us the strength to rise up as courageous soldiers doing the Lord's will.

Joel 3:10 Beat your plowshares into swords, and your pruning hooks into spears: let the weak say, I am strong.

NOT NEGOTIABLE

Proverbs 1:10 My son, if sinful men entice you, do not give in to them.

I have been asked many times how I was able to lose over 80 pounds over the last four years and keep it off. Also, how I was able to come back from the effects of a stroke in that same amount of time. I have explained on numerous occasions that I had to developer a 'Not Negotiable' attitude within the lifestyle changes I made. My decisions to stick to what God had been teaching me during my time of healing and recovery is the difference maker in my life. Isa. 30:21a **Your own ears will hear Him. Right behind you a voice will say, "This is the way you should go."**

The hard choices I had to make - exercise every day and eat only real food - had to become a not negotiable stubbornness within my heart. I can eat whatever junk I want, but choose not to. I can lay around like a lump on a log, but I choose not to. I can justify and rationalize laziness in all areas of my life, but I say "No, this is not negotiable.

I will live and thank God for the second chance He gave me." I heard a character in a movie say, "Get busy with living, or get busy with dying." I decided this was good advice, and I decided to get busy with living. God willing, I will keep choosing life.

One of the reasons people slowly fall back into old bad habits is because they have let their guard down and negotiated their will away for the cravings being dangled before them. Compromising becomes a way of getting through the maze of countless decisions everyone has to make on a daily basis. Eventually, the body dictates what it wants and negotiates its' will away by reasoning that it is easier to just give up and lie down. This is a lie of the enemy of our soul. We can do better than submit to mediocrity.

When Satan was tempting Jesus in the desert, he tried to get Jesus to negotiate outside of God's plan for the redemption of man. Matt. 4:8 **Again, the devil took him up into an exceeding high mountain, and showed him all the kingdoms of the world, and the glory of them;** 9 **and saith unto him, All these things will I give thee, if thou wilt fall down and worship me.**

God's plan was a mystery hidden in Christ. Satan's plan was pathetically obvious and short-sighted, as usual.

Even though the devil recognized Jesus as the son of God, he did not really believe Jesus could win the redemption of man from the position of a human being. Satan was used to seeing man compromise and see him/her negotiate their will down to a piece of bread or anything prohibiting a life-threatening situation. Job 2:4 **Satan replied to the LORD, "Skin for skin! A man will give up everything he has to save his life."** The devil was not accustomed to having someone step forward with a not negotiable heart. Jesus was that man and the one to demonstrate to us how to overcome the temptations of the evil one - through God's word and our not negotiable will.

When we come to the realization that we have been paid for in full through the blood of Jesus, by the Lord of lords and the King of kings, we too will develop a heart attitude of a not negotiable standard. When we believe we can overcome the cheap and disingenuous negotiations of the devil, we will not fear raising our banner Jehovah-Nissi - The Lord is my banner. Ex. 17:15 **Moses built**

an altar there and named it Yahweh-Nissi (which means "the LORD is my banner").

When we finally decide to wave the banner of our God high and forcefully over our heads, we will become men and women of God who will not negotiate with sin. When life offers us cheap short-cuts around the will of God, we will bravely say, "No! This is not negotiable." I admonish each one of you who reads this to give it an honest try. Shout from your heart, "I have been paid for in full by Jesus my Lord and my will is not negotiable!" Blessings, Saints.

COURAGE FOR THE DAY

Proverbs 18:10 The name of the LORD is a strong tower: the righteous run into it, and is safe.

John Wayne said, "Courage was being scared to death but saddling up anyway."

In the Scriptures, God admonishes us to be courageous, or to take up some courage for the task at hand. Josh. 1:7 **Only be strong and very courageous, that you may observe to do according to all the law which Moses My servant commanded you; do not turn from it to the right hand or to the left, that you may prosper wherever you go.** Being courageous is a choice and an obedient action on our part. It seems like we have to step up to the plate, be courageous, and believe that God will honor our courage by faith.

When we look around us and see all the terrible world events taking place day after day, we can become disheartened by all the bad news. If we keep focusing on all that is wrong in the world, we will be overcome with discouragement and forget the blessings of God in our lives. The Lord is mighty and strong and has overcome the world. However, we must stay close to God and run to Him in times of weakness. Prov. 18:10 **The name of the LORD is a strong tower: the righteous run into it, and is safe.**

The Lord is continually trying to lift us up and out of our circumstances so that we can experience the power of victory through Christ. God asks us to be of good courage and keep going forward toward our eternal reward. Psalm 31:24 **Be of good courage, and he shall strengthen your heart, all ye that hope in the LORD.**

We often look for some way of staying courageous in God, but all we have to do is be courageous one day at a time. God asks that we find the courage needed for the day we are living in. Matt. 6:34 **So do not worry about tomorrow; for tomorrow will care for itself. Each day has enough trouble of its own.** If we can find the courage for the task of the day, we will overcome the plan of the enemy.

Hezekiah was facing a formidable foe from Assyria. The people under King Hezekiah were outnumbered and out-flanked on all sides. Hezekiah had to remind the people that God was on their side; therefore, they could take courage in that fact. Once they got their eyes on the solution and took their eyes off of the threat, courage began to flow out of their faith. 2Chron. 32:7 **Be strong and courageous, be not afraid nor dismayed for the king of Assyria, nor for all the multitude that is with him: for there be more with us than with him:** 8 **With him is an arm of flesh; but with us is the LORD our God to help us, and to fight our battles. And the people rested themselves upon the words of Hezekiah king of Judah.** I love the last part of that verse. "And the people rested themselves upon the words of Hezekiah king of Judah." Wow! Rest came from their faith and was poured into courage.

It will take real courage for us to make it in this life. Every day brings different challenges. We will need a constant supply of God-like courage to help us choose what is right and to do what is asked of us by the Holy Spirit. The world is getting bolder and outrageous in behavior and louder in demanding more sinful rights. We will need the courage of God in our hearts to speak out in love and be a blessing on this earth. The name of the Lord is a strong tower. We can take courage for the day in that fact. Take courage, saints! God is good.

WE CAN DO BETTER

Proverbs 15:17 Better is a dinner of herbs where love is than a fattened ox and hatred with it.

We can do better, but we have to want to. We can do better. We can be better at who we are and how we grow as individuals. However, we will have to want it and put action to it much more than just saying it with no heartfelt desire of changing.

There was a man whose name was Jabez. We get an idea of his life being rough and not fair because his mother named him after her sorrowful delivery while giving birth. Furthermore, he seems to have had brothers who were not honoring toward him. 1Chron. 4:9 **And Jabez was more honourable than his brethren: and his mother called his name Jabez, saying, Because I bare him with sorrow.** Jabez was named after a bad experience. Love seemed to be missing in his life. Prov. 15:17 **Better is a dinner of herbs where love is than a fattened ox and hatred with it.**

Many people use excuses for their dysfunctional

upbringing and poor circumstances to determine their poor choices in life. Jails are full of people who say they just could not make anything of their lives because of their poverty, alcoholic and drug-addicted family members, and poor choices of friends. Escape from these problems was impossible; jail was inevitable. This is the tale they tell continually. I do agree that hard environments can cause a trend of lawlessness and self-esteem difficulties when there are no honorable role models. However, the final choices we make are still our own. We have to want change in order to change. We cannot just wish upon a star and voila, it's done.

Jabez wanted something more than what he had. He felt things could be better. He felt he could do better, so he went to God in faith with a simple prayer. 1Chron. 4:10 **He was the one who prayed to the God of Israel, "Oh, that you would bless me and expand my territory! Please be with me in all that I do, and keep me from all trouble and pain!" And God granted him his request.** Jabez was dealing with troubles and pain. It caused him to consider God and not choose a destructive life path as some of his brothers did. Jabez wanted what everyone wants, but he had the sense to go to the Creator of life and ask for it.

Maybe you feel stuck in a dead-end job with no hope for the future. Then ask God for the courage to want to change who you are and not fear thinking you could do better. You may have lived with a just-get-by life and you have a dream that things could be better. Ask God to bless you and expand your territory. Even our Lord Jesus wanted a better covenant for us. He did it with the work of the cross. Heb. 8:6 **But as it is, Christ has obtained a ministry that is as much more excellent than the old as the covenant he mediates is better, since it is enacted on better promises.** The Lord's heart for us was and is for something better. We just have to say, "Yes Lord, I want that better covenant and all the blessings that come with it."

We can all do better, because the Lord of glory lives within us. We were once dead in our trespasses and sins, but no longer do we have to stay there. We have been delivered from those shackles. We can now move forward with Christ, overcoming the troubles and the pain that once had control of our lives.

Like Jabez, we can ask God to give us more territory and a larger sphere of influence in the kingdom of God, plus a better life purpose. We just have to want it with all of our hearts. That is the true depth of the prayer Jabez released by faith. He wanted something much more and the plea of his heart was heard on high. Jabez was serious and meant what he was asking. How serious are you about changing your destiny, or is it all just talk?

No, Saints. We can do better. There comes a time when we must realize that when we come to God with a simple and honest request, He will hear us. It is time to believe that life can be better. Eph. 3:20 **Now all glory to God, who is able, through his mighty power at work within us, to accomplish infinitely more than we might ask or think.** Blessings to you.

THE LAST HURRAH

Proverbs 29:26 Many seek the ruler's favour; but every man's judgment comes from the LORD.

I was thinking about the words that were recorded about one of the kings who ruled over Judah. Amaziah reigned twenty-nine years in Jerusalem and did some good things for the country and the people. However, the point God brings out about him is not that flattering. 2Chron. 25:2 **And he did that which was right in the sight of the LORD, but not with a perfect heart.**

In other words, "He was just so so." Not quite the last thing you want God to say about your life and existence while you were here on earth living out God's assignment for your life. He did things right, but his heart just wasn't into it. His heart was not submitted to God.

The words "Well done faithful servant" may not be what is heard on that day for many who have taken the same attitude toward God and life. Col. 3:23 **And whatsoever ye do, do it heartily,**

as to the Lord, and not unto men. Making our last hurrah count for God and His kingdom can only be done through God's salvation plan and His only. God the Father has given us Jesus as our saving Lord. Acts 4:12 **Salvation is found in no one else, for there is no other name under heaven given to mankind by which we must be saved.**

We have all heard of people who try to make their last years on earth count for something. Some try to fulfill a bucket-list of things and events that must get done before passing. Others start the long arduous journey of apologizing to those they hurt throughout their careless lives. Some travel the world looking for the guru that can give them the assurance they desperately need to allay their fears of an unknown eternity. Many get involved in doing good works to gather ingratiating points for the day they stand before God, hoping it will be enough to pass muster so to speak. Prov. 29:26 **Many seek the ruler's favour; but every man's judgment comes from the LORD.**

However, like King Amaziah these people are doing these things without the heart of God, not having God in their hearts as they go about finalizing their reason for living. Their last hurrah may end up being a whimper in the eyes of God. The people themselves may think what they are doing is great, but not if Christ is not leading their charge.

I found an interesting small verse in the book of Romans. The Apostle Paul is leaving instructions to the people in Christ. One of the things he says to do is "Greet Apelles." What he says has great weight. Rom. 16:10a **Greet Apelles, tested and approved in Christ.** Another translation says, "**Greet Apelles, whose fidelity to Christ has stood the test.**"

Now that is a last hurrah. To have these words written about your character far outweighs the comment King Amaziah got. Imagine having these words beside your recorded name in the word of God; tested and approved in Christ. I do not know what Apelles did for a living or what he did for the church, but these words sure do inspire me to be like-minded.

The history of God's (ekklesia) church is being written and recorded by God to this day. Wouldn't it be nice to hear these words alongside of "Well done, faithful servant, for you have been tested and approved in Christ." As I become more intentional in the work and ministry of the Lord, I am leaning toward having the words Apelles is known for over my life. I would like my last hurrah on this earth to be noticed by God for the right reason. Not because I was half-hearted, but rather I had been tested and approved in Christ. By the grace of God, may it be so. In Jesus name.

SELF-ANALYSIS

Proverbs 20:6 Most men will proclaim every one his own goodness: but a faithful man who can find?

Norm Sawyer said, "While working out at the gym, I have never met a mirror I didn't like."

Self-analysis can be quite biased when trying to proclaim our own goodness and personal qualities. It takes an honest probe from the Holy Spirit - who is purity personified - to point out or convict us of who we are in life. John 16:8 **And when He comes, He will convict the world of its sin, and of God's righteousness, and of the coming judgment.**

When working hand in hand with the Lord - self-analysis is possible. However, the brutal truth of discovering things about ourselves that we do not like can be disheartening. We will have to trust the final analysis of God's perfect evaluation of what our hearts will need to be in relationship with God. Amos 3:3 **Can two walk together, except they be agreed?** Thankfully the transforming work Christ has done within us far exceeds any of our own efforts or self-evaluation.

When we release our will and walk by faith, the healing Christ brings into our life will be a complete and lasting work. This God-inspired work will bring maturity to our souls. Jude 1:24 **Now all glory to God, who is able to keep you from falling away and will bring you with great joy into his glorious presence without a single fault.** God knows what the inner man needs and how the blood of Jesus Christ can fix, mend, and heal our soul, mind, and lives.

When we look in the mirror and don't like what we see, we clean up and change clothes. We adjust this and that till we are acceptable. When we look into the mirror of God's word, we allow God to do the adjusting of what He sees needing Holy intervention until we have the peace of the Lord ruling in our hearts. Phil. 4:7 **And the peace of God, which surpasses all understanding, will guard your hearts and your minds in Christ Jesus.**

Self-analysis is only as good as the character within a person. If a person is of Godly character, then hopefully God's word will be used to correct their heart. A person of poor character is another story. Prov. 20:6a **Most men will proclaim every one his own goodness.** For a lot of people, the biased proclamation continues into self-deception.

I am so grateful the Lord sent us the Holy Spirit to continually lead us and guide us into all truth that is profitable for our soul to become who God created us to be in Him. 2Tim. 3:16 **All Scripture is God-breathed and is useful for instruction, for conviction, for correction, and for training in righteousness,** 17 **so that the man of God may be complete, having been fully equipped toward every good work.** We truly are God's workmanship. It is only when we let Him analyze our lives that we will come forth as gold purified by the Lord.

The next time we are looking in the mirror and are adjusting this and that, we can smile and know within our spirit that God is doing the same thing within our soul for His glory. John 16:13a **But when He the, Spirit of truth, shall come, He will guide you into all the truth.** Blessings to us all.

IF YOU SAY

Proverbs 18:21 Death and life are in the power of the tongue: and they that love it shall eat the fruit thereof.

We read in the old testament of Samuel, a Judge and Prophet to Israel. There is a noteworthy statement made about him as he grew up in his calling, 1Sam. 3:19 **And Samuel grew, and the LORD was with him, and did let none of his words fall to the ground.** All his words had spiritual weight to them. What he said in the name of God would come to pass.

Many in the church today express the desire to have the same type of anointing. The truth is, we do have that anointing. Jesus said in Mark 11:22 **And Jesus answering saith unto them, Have faith in God.** 23 **For verily I say unto you, That whosoever shall say unto this mountain, Be thou removed, and be thou cast into the sea; and shall not doubt in his heart, but shall believe that those things which he saith shall come to pass; he shall have whatsoever he**

saith.

As the Lord says in this verse, what and how we say things is important for the expected result of our prayers. I heard Kenneth Copeland say, "People can have whatever they say, but they have been saying what they have."

Solomon, the wisest and richest man, saw the result of his proverb working in people's lives day by day. The conclusion was death and life is in the power of the tongue. They would get the fruit of their words spoken by faith or unbelief. James was concerned about how we use our words. James 3:10 **Out of the same mouth proceeds blessing and cursing. My brethren, these things ought not so to be.**

I agree with James that these things ought not to be. We should use the authority of what we say to bless and bring prosperity for the growth of the Kingdom of God. We should be talking like Jesus who gave us His mandate to go into all the world and minister His word so that all may come to the knowledge of Jesus Christ. How could God send us into the world, prowled by wolves, without there being an authority in our faith spoken words? Jesus said that He would send the Holy Spirit so that we could speak with Christ's authority.

John 17:20 **Neither pray I for these alone, but for them also which shall believe on me through their word.** What word was that? The everyday words that Jesus used that never fell to the ground. Words of faith, spoken and said with authority.

Mary must have noticed the way Jesus spoke and the results of His words as he grew in stature of manhood. At the wedding in Cana, Mary says something incredible to the servants. John 2:5 **His mother saith unto the servants, Whatsoever he says unto you, do it.** Whatever HE SAYS, do it. Since we are to do what Jesus says, then when the Lord says to say to the mountains that are in our lives to be removed, then it is time to do what He says. Say it from a heart of faith.

Paul exhorts us in the Epistle of Ephesians to put on the armour of God, plus, pray with all manner of prayer; then he asked for a specific prayer request. Eph. 6:19 **And for me, that utterance may be given unto me, that I may open my mouth boldly, to make known the mystery of the gospel.** Paul wanted his words to have an impact on those who would hear and that his words would not fall to the ground.

I find it hard to understand why we do not take this admonition from the Lord to our hearts and believe His word on this matter. Why is it so hard to believe what God is saying here? He says to say to the mountain, "Be removed and it will obey us." Num. 23:19a **God is not a man that He should lie.**

If the Lord says that death and life is in the power of the tongue, then that is our starting point. We use our faith-filled words that contain the power of God and we say, "Mountains be removed." Christ said it, therefore, so be it!

LIKE ME ON

Proverbs 19:8 To acquire wisdom is to love yourself; people who cherish understanding will prosper.

Please, someone out there, "like me!" Like me on Facebook, Youtube, Soundcloud or on anything, but please - just like me. Are you living your life for the sake of a like? We have to like ourselves and be comfortable in our own skin so we can be happy with who God made us to be. Mark 12:31a **Love your neighbor as yourself.**

I feel sorry for a lot of neighbours if they are being loved as people love themselves. With so many people struggling with personality issues, body image acceptance and low self-confidence in who they are, their neighbours must be neurotic by now if they are being loved in the same way.

Man's approval is fine, but God's approval is paramount for our well-being. God has already accepted us through His son Jesus Christ. All we have to do is accept the sacrifice that God says is perfect; therefore, those who are in Christ are eternally liked, so to speak, and accepted for who they are.

When we accept Jesus as Lord, we now live a life that works toward pleasing our Lord. Then by God's grace, we begin to mature into a place where we accept ourselves and each other. Man's ways of acceptance just cannot do what God has done for us through Jesus our Savior. Acts 4:12 **And there is salvation in no one else; for there is no other name under heaven that has been given among men by which we must be saved.**

Many may feel what my sister in the Lord, Jami Rogers, said. "I think it's a pretty good call that I'm in a major testing zone, and someone keeps giving me more tests than I have pencils for!" Are you overwhelmed with man's standard of passing the grade? The tests, qualifications, and endurance races that man puts other people through to be accepted and liked is flawed at best and downright impossible to achieve at worst. Trying to pass these tests will result in burnout. Psalm 69:3a **I am exhausted from shouting for help; my throat is sore.**

The like-me-meter that man has implemented

for worldwide approval is a moving target from day-to-day, depending on the whims of so-called aficionados of pop-culture and those with varying political stripes. We cannot get our self-worth from people who have no self-worth themselves.

People cannot give away what they do not have! Otherwise, we would be jumping through man-made hoops of impossible reality all day long. If we depend on man's likes to be at peace within ourselves, we will be continually in a place of being blackballed because the only color of balls available in the ballot box is black. A no-win scenario. Hag. 1:9a **You expected much, but then it amounted to little.**

Let us put our life efforts into pleasing God and find ourselves in His book of likes. Mal. 3:16 **Then those who feared the LORD spoke with one another. The LORD paid attention and heard them, and a book of remembrance was written before him of those who feared the LORD and esteemed his name.**

I came into the Lord's presence this morning wearing my comfortable slippers, bright flannel shirt, and plain pants. I was accepted. I had a heart full of concerns, questions, and praise. I was pacified and strengthened in the Lord's grace. As the Proverb says, **"To acquire wisdom is to love yourself."**

I reckon I could say my day got started with some love and a blessed like. By God's grace, I am full of thanks for His faithfulness toward me. I know that I am loved, favored, and liked by almighty God. Wow! I will take that any day. Psalm 92:2 **To declare Your lovingkindness in the morning and Your faithfulness by night.** More than a like, God loves you. Blessings.

GETTING IT

Proverbs 1:6 To understand a proverb, and the interpretation; the words of the wise, and their dark sayings.

Eureka! Wow, that makes sense. Ah ha, I get it! What a flash of honest joy it is when the Holy Spirit finally gets through to our hearts and we see clearly what God was nurturing within us. That blessed and assured moment of spiritual clarity that we know, that we know, the Lord has hit home and we get it. In that heart smiling moment of relationship with Christ, there is no better feeling or high on earth that can compare.

The reality that we know there is nothing that can interfere with the closeness we have with God right then and there is worth life itself. Rom. 8:38 **For I am persuaded, that neither death, nor life, nor angels, nor principalities, nor powers, nor things present, nor things to come,** 39 **Nor height, nor depth, nor any other creature, shall be able to separate us from the love of God, which is in Christ Jesus**

our Lord.

In January of 2014, I was praying out of frustration and asking God for answers on difficult things I was going through. I was praying, "I need a real answer here Lord and not one of those Yea! Behold! things, but something in plain English." I was not being rude but asking in real earnestness, because I wanted real answers I could understand and follow. I stood there in quiet surrender to what God would say. Hab. 2:1 **I will stand my watch and set myself on the rampart, and watch to see what He will say to me, and what I will answer when I am corrected.**

I could have fallen over when I thought I heard this in my spirit. "Build a banqueting table!" "A what?" I said. In quietness of spirit, again, I thought I heard, "Build a banqueting table." As strange as it was, from that moment on I had a desire to build a banqueting table. I started coming across different types of wood people gave me. I also found wood on the slag heap at a sawmill. In my backyard in the warm days of spring, I started putting a table together from different types and sizes of wood. I eventually built a farmer's banqueting table that was seven feet long by three feet wide.

It had a cedar top with pine panel legs, spruce brackets at the footing, douglas-fir braces under the top, and a large ash wood brace on the bottom. Why the different types of wood? The simple answer. It's what I had to work with. As I was sanding and finishing the table project, I was amazed at the beauty of it with its wormhole scars and dark colored knots. Wood grain designs of different shades meandered through the table top. The beauty of the wood just spoke of God's creation and diversity. Isa. 55:12b **And all the trees of the field shall clap their hands.**

I was gushing out words of joy to my God about the beauty of the table's finished look and said, "I venture to say, Lord, that there is not another table like it in the universe. I love the way it turned out with all its numerous flaws, imperfections and genuine scarring. I love the way the wood feels with its lines of textured grain. I just love the way this table turned out. It is so unique." Then with a thunderous voice, I heard, "JUST LIKE YOU!"

I could have sworn the neighbourhood heard that voice. It was loud and right over me. The hair on the back of my neck was up and tingling. With loud exaltation in a perfect moment of clarity, I said, "I get it, Lord. So that's what you were trying to say to me back there in January when I was praying in frustration." I am unique! I venture to say there is no one like me in this universe, just like everyone who is reading this. You are so unique. God loves your uniqueness, because He made you that way. Wow! What a word in its season.

Yes, we might have a few wormholes, nicks, and knots distorting our looks but that does not matter. God made you and me unique to Himself. We need to embrace the individual love God has given each one of us. Psalm 139:14 **Thank you for making me so wonderfully complex! Your workmanship is marvelous, how well I know it.**

There is an intimate moment when Jesus is talking with the Apostle Peter. Jesus asks Peter, "Who do the people say I am, and who do you say I am Peter?" Peter gives Him this answer. Matt. 16:16 **And Simon Peter answered and said, Thou art the Christ, the Son of the living God.**17 **And Jesus answered and said**

unto him, Blessed art thou, Simon Barjona: for flesh and blood hath not revealed it unto thee, but my Father which is in heaven.

When things are revealed to us by our heavenly Father and we get it and respond to the truth of it, then we are a blessed people. We experience wonderful moments of understanding who we are and why we are. We are uniquely God's workmanship created for his pleasure Rev. 4:11 **You are worthy, O Lord our God, to receive glory and honor and power. For you created all things, and they exist because you created what you pleased.**

The interesting thing is that I cannot remember what the reason was for the frustration that made me so intense to pray back then in January. I don't remember what it was about. I can only remember the joy of the project and finding out I am as unique as each one of you. We are uniquely owned and loved by God and He pours out His goodness toward us. I get it! Praise The Lord.

BULLDOG TENACITY

Proverbs 24:16 Though a righteous person falls seven times, they will get up, but the wicked will stumble into ruin.

"I cut this board three times and it is still too short!" The foolishness of this line is apparent, even though it is funny. Some people live their lives within the same manner of activity. They repeat the failure that is obvious to many over and over and they complain that the result is the same.

Others spend their grocery money on cigarettes, alcohol and junk, and then complain there is no money for food, rent, and payments due. Some hang out with abusive and dishonorable people and complain of unfaithful friends. They do the same things over again, claiming to be right in their actions. Prov. 12:15 **Fools think their own way is right, but the wise listen to others.**

You cannot defeat the devil you like to play with. You cannot beat the sin you enjoy participating in. Until you develop a bulldog tenacity and say

"No" to the sin that so easily besets your life, you will remain captive to the mess you are in.

Until you pick up the weapons of God's grace and power with the mindset to use them, you will not be able to defeat the bondage holding you back. 2Cor. 10:4 **The weapons we fight with are not the weapons of the world. On the contrary, they have divine power to demolish strongholds.** 5 **We demolish arguments and every pretension that sets itself up against the knowledge of God, and we take captive every thought to make it obedient to Christ.**

Yes, scripture says we can do all things through Christ who strengthens us. It is true that God will give us the strength and ability to overcome every temptation that comes our way; however, we will have to step forward by faith and decide to be tenacious about going forward in righteousness.

We will have to yoke our heart to the Lord's and walk together, not contrary to each other. Matt. 11:30 **For the yoke I will give you is easy, and the load I will put on you is light.** The yoke may be easy and light, but it is a yoke nonetheless. It will take a bulldog tenacity to remain and walk with Christ through all of life for now and evermore. We cannot put God's grace and yoke on and take it off at the whim of our fickle feelings. This relationship with our Lord is permanent and eternal, not an on again and off again soap opera.

Elijah was looking for someone to take his mantel and came across Elisha who had a bulldog tenacity. 1Kings 19:19a **So he departed from there, and found Elisha the son of Shaphat, who was plowing with twelve yoke of oxen before him, and he was with the twelfth**. Elisha plowed with twelve yoke of oxen. The amount of strength and will power it took to control such a large bullock team is understated in this scripture verse. The brute force and work it took for one man to control these big beasts of burden would have taken talent, patience, and tenacity to keep the row being plowed straight.

It is interesting the attitude and character that came out of Elisha when Elijah asked him what he wanted before Elijah was taken away. Elisha wanted a double portion of the anointing that was on Elijah. 2Kings 2:9 **After they had crossed over, Elijah said to Elisha, "Tell me, what can I do for you before I am taken away**

from you?" "Please, let me inherit a double portion of your spirit," Elisha replied.

Elisha got what he asked for. I believe it was the bulldog tenacity of character that helped Elisha receive the promise. He was used to working hard and doing it right.

A bulldog tenacity is something that is learned and acquired. You must exercise your faith day by day and pick yourself up with the Lord's help when you fall, fail, and mess up. Prov. 24:16 **Though a righteous person falls seven times, they will get up, but the wicked will stumble into ruin.**

Elisha had the right stuff because he wanted more of God on God's terms. God's heart is that none of us perish because of our own foolish ways, but He wants us to grow up and be tenaciously solid in His love and gift of eternal life through Jesus our Lord. Blessings.

USE BEFORE DATE

Proverbs 2:3 Yea, if thou cry after knowledge, and lift up thy voice for understanding.

There have been a few deaths this past month of people in the assembly I am a member of. I was reading the life and death dates of these people who have passed on. A thought came to me as I read these dates. The days of our lives are numbered and in the hands of our God. Job 14:5 **You have decided the length of our lives. You know how many months we will live, and we are not given a minute longer**.

I suddenly saw the date of death as a Use Before Date, because there will be no more use on earth after the date of death. I could see the Lord going through His list of people that are His servants, and since God knows the number of our days He had to implement our use before the Use Before Date ran out. A strange thought, but in the moment it made a quirky sense to me.

I have an allotted time on this earth to bring glory to His name and be a blessing that represents the wonder and all infinite love that our Lord has for mankind. Time is truly short. I thought, "What have I done in the time given to me? What is left to do before my Use Before Date expires?" James 4:14 **Whereas ye know not what shall be on the morrow. For what is your life? It is even a vapour, that appears for a little time, and then vanishes away.**

I have to say these questions brought on some deep thought and consternation to my heart. What do I do with the time left to me? Wait a minute here. Am I stressing about the future in the Lord? Where did my peace go? I had it until I started this line of thinking.

The word of God says not to worry or stress about tomorrow. Matt. 6:34 **Therefore do not worry about tomorrow, for tomorrow will worry about its own things. Sufficient for the day is its own trouble.** I have been told this by numerous doctors that I have seen over the last six months. They say, "You need to get stress out of your life" because they are convinced that is what caused the atrial fibrillation I am struggling with right now.

I have thanked them for this insight. I have

asked all these learned medical practitioners this same question, "What does a stress-free life look like?" As they stress over the answer, I can see that no one knows. They all have these canned answers and ideas of what they think it looks like, but no one really knows. Most people are suffering from some sort of stress related ill-effect. Everyone knows they need to de-stress, but what does it look like?

We live in a world that has pushed the over-consumptive populations to operate at maximum stress for the productivity needed to keep the stress levels moving along. People are working and trying to live from a position of fear and stress. They are afraid of losing out. When I ask them what they are afraid of losing out on, they are not quite sure because they are too stressed to think it through.

No wonder so many well-meaning people are burning out and expiring before their actual Use Before Date is due. Luke 21:26 **Men's hearts failing them for fear, and for looking after those things which are coming on the earth: for the powers of heaven shall be shaken.**

I would like to think that my Use Before Date

is way out there in the long distance future. If it isn't, then it is what it is and stressing about it will only bring that date closer. Kind of a lose-lose situation. So I need to implement what the Lord says about all my stressing out in life. Matt. 6:31 **Therefore do not worry, saying, "What shall we eat?" or "What shall we drink?" or "What shall we wear?"** 32 **These things dominate the thoughts of unbelievers, but your heavenly Father already knows all your needs.**

My heavenly Father knows what I need to live a blessed life and overcome stress. Jesus is saying, "This is what it looks like to start living a stress-free life." I am to take my eyes off of what is stressing me to the point of illness and change my focus to what Jesus focused on. Matt. 6:3 **Seek the Kingdom of God above all else, and live righteously, and he will give you everything you need.**

Healing is what I need. The kingdom of God is where the answers are for now and throughout eternity. I don't believe another prescription of beta blockers, blood thinners, antidepressants, and blood pressure pills will bring down the stress in people's lives. As a matter of fact, I think the stress levels will go way up when they see the pharmaceutical bills piling up month after month. Plus the reality of no real relief from stress taking place, but only a bunch of side effects from the pills that will cause more stress. What a vicious circle. Oh God, thank you, that you have the answer.

Lord, Jesus, I can only ask you to keep showing me and my brothers and sisters in Christ what a stress-free life looks like. As I seek you and your kingdom first, may the eye of my understanding open up and see what steps to take day after day. May this action extend my Use Before Date to give me the ability to keep being a blessing in the Kingdom of God. John 14:27 **Peace I leave with you, My peace I give to you; not as the world gives do I give to you. Let not your heart be troubled, neither let it be afraid.** Amen and amen!

PART FOUR:

QUESTIONS FOR UNDERSTANDING

1. *What did you learn in this section of the book?*
2. *What surprised you the most?*
3. *What subject(s) spoke to your heart?*
4. *Did the material that you read help you understand the subject(s) more or less?*
5. *What topics are important to you? Why?*
6. *How do these articles relate to you?*
7. *After reading this section of the book, what will you change in your life?*

PART FIVE:

TRUTHFULNESS

The leaves of the trees are truthful in their display when declaring the state of seasons, health, and growth. Matthew 7:20 So then, you will recognize them by their fruit.

STOLEN VALOR

Proverbs 13:7 One person pretends to be rich, yet has nothing; another pretends to be poor, yet has great wealth.

There are people pretending to be something they are not in order to steal what is not theirs. Prov. 13:7a **One person pretends to be rich, yet has nothing.** This is a problem that military veterans have come across as they are catching people who have never served in the military pretending to be soldiers.

These people dress in full uniform, pretending and scamming for the benefits allowed to veterans, or stealing the admiration and respect due to those who have truly served their country. To me, this is low when it comes to scamming. It runs alongside of ripping off the elderly.

Interestingly, Satan has been doing the same thing and deceiving many into thinking he is worthy of the people's admiration and respect. He is always trying to steal God's glory and followers. The devil scams through deception, saying he has some good things that will fulfill our lives. Satan has been scamming throughout history, pretending to be an angel of light. 2Cor. 11:14 **And no wonder, for Satan himself masquerades as an angel of light.**

Is it any wonder people are doing the same thing? They are acting out, just like the one who had been influencing them; the devil. Jesus said the devil is a destroyer and a liar. The Lord says the devil has always been that way from the beginning. John 8:44 **You are of your father the Devil, and you want to carry out your father's desires. He was a murderer from the beginning and has not stood in the truth, because there is no truth in him. When he tells a lie, he speaks from his own nature, because he is a liar and the father of liars.**

There is also disappointment when we find out athletes have been stripped of their medals, because they pretended to be competing on an even level. We often find out they are chemically enhanced to perform beyond their ability. They accept the glory and medal in a ceremony of valor, only to be stripped of the medal of distinction later on when they are found out, through tests, that they were cheating. The acid test of life showed the world they did not have any valor in their character.

It is interesting that the Apostle Paul compares us to who we are in Christ as soldiers in the Lord's army. We have been recruited by Jesus Christ into the kingdom of God and our attention should be on the affairs of the kingdom. 2Tim. 2:4 **No one serving as a soldier gets entangled in the concerns of civilian life; he seeks to please the recruiter.** Our valor is found at the cross of Jesus Christ and in His blood only. 2Tim. 2:3 **Thou therefore endure hardness, as a good soldier of Jesus Christ.**

We do not have to seek or take the valor of any other soldier in the body of Christ, because we have all been given our assignments in the Lord. Some are chosen to do great things; others are chosen to hold down the fort, so to speak, but nonetheless, we are all chosen in Christ. 2Tim. 2:20 **In a large house there are articles not only of gold and silver, but also of wood and clay; some are for special purposes and some for common use.**

We have been posted here on earth, in the body

of Christ, to be a hand extended in welcoming those who will become believers in Christ. We are the body, and no one is without use or influence. 1Cor. 12:21 **The eye cannot say to the hand, "I don't need you!" And the head cannot say to the feet, "I don't need you!"** 22 **On the contrary, those parts of the body that seem to be weaker are indispensable.**

We do not have to pretend to be Christians; we just have to be one who loves and obeys the Lord. God will call out our valor, as He did with Gideon. Judges 6:12 **And the angel of the LORD appeared unto him, and said unto him, The LORD is with thee, thou mighty man of valor.** Gideon did not feel so great a person, but God saw the potential in him as He saw it in you when He saved you. Don't let the enemy of our soul steal our God-given valor that was paid for in full by Jesus on the cross. Be valiant men and women of God. Amen.

LEAKY SOULS

Proverbs 19:15 Slothfulness casts into a deep sleep; and an idle soul shall suffer hunger.

Ecclesiastes 10:18 **Through laziness, the rafters sag; because of idle hands, the house leaks.**

We sometimes think we have autonomy from the commands of the Lord because we have walked with the Lord for a long time. We rationalize that some of the commands and directions in the word of God do not apply to us anymore. We think we have earned some kind of carte blanche that exempts us from the common man's rules, so to speak. We begin to leak in our soul by thinking we have graduated to some level of autonomy beyond the reach of God's word. After all, "I am He who worships thee!"

Believing we have freedom from external control or influence can lead to a leaky soul. We are the house of the Lord. We have to ask ourselves if we are leaking. Is your soul leaking? Do the rafters of your character sag? Is this why we sometimes have an unfulfilled hunger in our soul?

The thing we have to realize is that the older we get in our walk with the Lord, the more God expects us to live by His word through His grace. Heb. 5:12 **You have been believers so long now that you ought to be teaching others. Instead, you need someone to teach you again the basic things about God's word. You are like babies who need milk and cannot eat solid food.**

Unlike the world system when someone gets perks or a promotion and a title beside their name, they sometimes tend to take more liberties and advantages because they are now upper management. It does not work that way in the kingdom of God. The more senior you get, so to speak, the more diligence and forthrightness is expected of you.

We have seen this type of unfortunate scene take place over the years. A mighty man of God grows and becomes known world-wide and the ministry he is expanding is doing great things in the kingdom of God. Then he or she gets sidelined with a scandal of adultery or embezzlement, and sometimes something worse. Is there forgiveness for these misled ministers who are now dealing with a leaky soul? Absolutely! 1John 1:9 **If we confess our sins, he is faithful and just to forgive us our sins, and to cleanse us from all unrighteousness.** There is complete forgiveness if they ask for it by faith and repent of their sin, but the damage to the ministry is often irreparable.

The Apostle Peter was having a hard time with one of these leaky soul problems. Jesus had said the time was coming when He would go to Jerusalem and would suffer at the hands of the spiritual leaders. Matt. 16:22 **But Peter took him aside and began to reprimand him for saying such things. "Heaven forbid, Lord," he said. "This will never happen to you!"** Imagine taking Jesus aside and reprimanding him! Peter's understanding of the Lord's ministry had become man-centered and not God-centered.

Peter forgot Jesus was there because of God's vision for the world. Even working with Jesus, it is possible to start leaking in one's soul and miss the mark as Peter did. Matt. 16:23 **Jesus turned to Peter and said, "Get away from me, Satan! You are a dangerous trap to me. You are**

seeing things merely from a human point of view, not from God's."

The word of God says that faith comes by hearing the word of God and also doing what it says. That is how we plug up the leaks and stay full of the Holy Spirit's oil. 2 Tim. 2:15 **Study to shew thyself approved unto God, a workman that needs not to be ashamed, rightly dividing the word of truth.** The word instructs us to study and be diligent in God's truth. This is a lifetime assignment and not something we can pick up over the weekend and it's all done. We will always have to make sure we are not leaking worldliness and becoming lazy in our walk with the Lord. Stay sharp, Saints.

WISDOM OF THE FOOLISH

Proverbs 1:22 How long, ye simple ones, will ye love simplicity? and the scorners delight in their scorning, and fools hate knowledge?

Bertrand Russell said, "Do not feel envious of the happiness of those who live in a fool's paradise, for only a fool will think that it is happiness."

How foolish can we be as a people and as individuals? Very foolish. Throughout history, we have seen nations become foolish collectively. These nations, along with the world, sit back and wonder how such foolishness could have happened on a national scale. In wonderment, they say, "How could this have happened?" Prov. 14:12 **There is a way that seems right to a man, but its end is the way to death.**

In my lifetime I have observed Cuba, North Korea, and the old USSR make slaves of their people. Through subterfuge and brutality of a few crafty people who moved in on the moral vacuum in leadership was able to take over. I realize I am stating an over simplistic view of these countries choices, as there are always historical events leading to the collapse or birth of an accepted ideology and government system. There is more to the stories of these countries and the people within them than I am presenting. I am simply thinking out loud, while wondering about these historical follies.

How did relatively free citizens use their free wills or voting rights to vote in a communist and ruthless government who would take away their freedoms and rights to vote? In some cases, laws for these same wayward citizens were created to make them forfeit their own thoughts and ideas as individuals. Unreasonable regulations dictated to the ordinary man by hubris buffoons who thought themselves wise and above their own regulations, laws, and rhetoric.

How foolish is that? Ignorance gone to seed on a national level. Yes, manipulation and brute force took place in these places to force people in the direction of these social abuses and insipid existence. In most cases, the people were promised nirvana, so to speak, if they went along with the political ruse. These sad events that went on are likely to repeat themselves.

Humanity will make these same choices throughout the coming years in different parts of the world. The wisdom of the foolish within the lost people of the world will continue as long as there is no change of heart within the crowds and nations. Eccl. 1:9 **What has been will be again, what has been done will be done again; there is nothing new under the sun.**

The choices of many in life accelerate this problem when he or she chooses to believe in nothing. When this becomes the common thread in the hearts of the people, then anything begins to sound good; even the declarations of the Godless. Psalm 14:1a **The fool says in his heart, "There is no God."**

The solution can come from each person if the gift of God is caught in their minds and hearts. In most cases, our desires in life are to attain liberty and freedom of choice. We all want better things for our children and society, plus we all want to have the freedom to live in peace. God provided this very thing through the love and sacrifice of Jesus. 2Cor. 3:17 **Now the Lord is the Spirit, and where the Spirit of the Lord is, there is**

freedom. John 8:32 **Then you will know the truth, and the truth will set you free.**

Someone might say I am oversimplifying the fix for all of mankind's ilks. No! I am not oversimplifying or making light of the complexities in the world. It is these complexities that attract the type of political vermin who bring in death-squads and fear to dominate and steal the hearts of the people. These political predators see a lack of faith in God and move in with their foolish idols and preach a doctrine of hate and revenge. Jude 1:4 **For there are certain men crept in unawares, who were before of old ordained to this condemnation, ungodly men, turning the grace of our God into lasciviousness, and denying the only Lord God, and our Lord Jesus Christ.**

God plainly declares His love for the world, because the gift of His Son is for everyone in the whole wide world. John 3:16 **For God so loved the world, that he gave his only begotten Son, that whosoever believes in him should not perish, but have everlasting life.** God, who is pure wisdom, knows Jesus is the answer for all of the world's wars, famines, diseases, and death.

God ought to know, as He is God and we are not.

God is saying Jesus can heal all the hearts in this earth. This is not a man-made theory, but a holy fact given to each human being as a gift from the creator of all. Reach out and accept it. All we have to do is say "Yes" to the Lord, and say "No" to foolishness.

There was a man walking on a sidewalk with a sandwich board. The front said, "I'm a fool for Jesus." The back part of the board said, "Whose fool are you?" Blessings to every person on this earth in Jesus name.

DON'T SAY IT

Proverbs 23:16 My innermost being will cheer when your lips say what is right.

William Shakespeare stated, "Give thy thoughts no tongue."

The good advice William Shakespeare was giving seemed to be "Keep your thoughts to yourself; act in a rational way." In this irrational world, that advice might be difficult. There are whole industries given to visual entertainment, scandal sheets, and call in radio shows devoted entirely to spewing one's thoughts and regurgitating them to the point of ad nauseam.

How often have we said something we wish wholeheartedly we could take the words back. Even after hearing that still small voice in our minds saying, "Don't say it!" But nonetheless, it got said, resulting in everything from divorce to libel court dates. They did not control the impulse in their minds. They gave free rein to their tongues, resulting in irreparable damage. James 3:5 **In the same way, the tongue is a small part of the**

body, but it boasts of great things. Consider how small a spark sets a great forest on fire.

I was spewing my thoughts in one situation and the lesson literally came home loud and clear. I had driven my wife to the airport. The scanners for boarding passes had just been introduced in the airport. I was having difficulty going through the prompts because the option I needed did not seem to come up. The elderly couple next to me were having a harder time with the scanners. They asked for assistance from an airline agent. With great exasperation and over-dramatic emphasis she blurted out, "Can't you read?"

Everyone in the area turned to look at the elderly couple who were paralyzed with embarrassment. I was indignant and red-faced at the discourtesy of this so-called service person. I got up to the counter and voiced my thoughts about this agent. What I said was not kind. What I did not know was that I had leaned on my bluetooth device in a way that it automatically called the last phone number that had been dialed. Everything I had said about this terrible airline agent was being recorded on the answering machine at the other end. Eccl. 10:20 **Do not revile the king even**

in your thoughts, or curse the rich in your bedroom, because a bird in the sky may carry your words, and a bird on the wing may report what you say.

The saving grace and mercy that came my way was the answering machine my words had been recorded on was the one at my own house. I was embarrassed at what I heard when I got home. The words of Jesus were without a doubt in my mind. Matt. 12:36 **But I tell you that everyone will have to give account on the day of judgment for every empty word they have spoken.**

Yes, my dear friends, I repented right there on the spot. Yes, there was a voice in my head saying, "Don't say it that way," but I did not listen. Since then, this event has become one of those family stories told once in a while as a life lesson. Chuckles and laughter sometimes come out in the retelling of my embarrassing display of unrighteousness. However, the lesson is clear, we are responsible for what we say and our words will be judged.

We will have to give an account of our verbiage given out on a daily basis. Col. 4:6 **Let**

your conversation be always full of grace, seasoned with salt, so that you may know how to answer everyone. There was a proper way to deal with the poor behavior of this airline agent. There are, in most cases, respectful ways of dealing with people behaving badly. I didn't do it with lips saying the right thing. The Lord's heart was not cheered with how I said it. Prov. 23:16 **My innermost being will cheer when your lips say what is right.**

As a parent, I have always hoped my sons would be men who speak kindly and respond the right way toward others. God, the Father, expects the same out of His children. As children of the most High God, we are ambassadors to the world - speaking the words of the Lord in love.

Love does sometimes have a hard word to say, but we can say it with grace, humility, and without being corrosive or argumentative. I am not as eloquent in speech as Mr. Shakespeare, but what he said makes sense. Heeding his advice would be a good thing for most of us on this earth to take on as a personal endeavor.

Guarding our tongue and listening to the voice that says "Don't say it" would be a good habit to develop in our hearts and minds. Prov. 25:11 **A word fitly spoken is like apples of gold in a setting of silver.** It's time to retool the way we say things. May God give us His grace to have lips to say what is right. Amen.

TRUTH OR OTHER

Proverbs 29:1 He, that being often reproved hardens his neck, shall suddenly be destroyed, and that without remedy.

I ministered in the prisons of New South Wales and Queensland, Australia for just over four years in the early nineteen-eighties. I was often taken aback by the generational family lines that were there in prison. In one case there was a young man who was telling me he had no choice that he was in jail. It was his unfortunate destiny that he would be a criminal. His reasoning at that encounter was his father was a criminal and his grandfather was one also. As a matter of fact, they were all incarcerated at the same time in different prisons around the state as we spoke.

He went on to say that his brother was headed in the same place. Ah, how sweet the conversation at Christmas dinner for this family. Talk about having to change the generational curse, or family traditions. Prov.16:25 **There is a way that seems right unto a man, but the end thereof are the**

ways of death. It sounded like a modern caste system that was being enforced by their own family values. What nonsense to believe this poor excuse for existence.

Being deceived and choosing to believe a lie is within our realm of choice. Deut. 30:19 **I call heaven and earth to record this day against you, that I have set before you life and death, blessing and cursing: therefore choose life, that both thou and thy seed may live.**

Being deceived may take some time to deal with. The deception may not be noticed until there are some issues coming up in our life that points to the deception and, thus, we repent. John 16:13a **Howbeit when he, the Spirit of truth, is come, he will guide you into all truth.**

Choosing to believe the lie is ignorance gone to seed. Gal. 3:1 **O foolish Galatians, who hath bewitched you, that ye should not obey the truth, before whose eyes Jesus Christ hath been evidently set forth, crucified among you?** As my blog friend Jami Rogers writes, "I tried to row the boat with the anchor in the water, then cried because of the struggle." How often do we find ourselves in that boat because of our choices? The answer is repent, change your mind.

God corrects those He loves. Heb. 12:6 **For whom the Lord love he chasten, and scourge every son whom he receives.** That is a hard concept for a nation of people who do not like being wrong. In their minds, correction seems intrusive and even insulting to some. This makes repentance harder than it really is. Yet, how will we come into the blessing of God if we insist on doing salvation our own way?

Repentance is a blessing, whether we believe it or not. Repentance simply means to change our minds on something God has been pointing at, or has His finger of conviction on. Repentance or changing our minds to do what God said to do is a healthy part of Christianity. It is the only way to live our Christianity. Isa. 30:21 **And thine ears shall hear a word behind thee, saying, This is the way, walk ye in it, when ye turn to the right hand, and when ye turn to the left.**

We read in the story of Cain and Abel how God had come to Cain and tried to get him to change his mind concerning the jealousy Cain was feeling because of his rejected sacrifice. God asks Cain a good question. Gen. 4:6 **And the**

LORD said unto Cain, "Why art thou wroth? and why is thy countenance fallen?"

Then God offers some very good advice and gentle prodding to repent about how he feels toward his brother. Gen. 4:7 **If thou does well, shalt thou not be accepted? and if thou does not well, sin lies at the door. And unto thee shall be his desire, and thou shalt rule over him.** As we know, the advice was ignored and a calamity of events leads to the first murder.

What could we change in our lives if we would just change our minds to what God is saying to our hearts? Eze. 18:32 **For I have no pleasure in the death of him that dies, saith the Lord GOD: wherefore turn yourselves, and live ye.** God takes no pleasure in our suffering in sin. He wants us to live by His truth and no other. Lord, help us have a heart of repentance. Amen.

SNARED BY YOUR WORDS

Proverbs 6:2 You are snared by the words of your mouth; you are taken by the words of your mouth.

Hafiz the Persian poet said, "The words you speak become the house you live in."

I once heard a country and western singer say that he had been experiencing in his everyday life everything he and his band had been singing about. He said, "I don't know why it is, but everything I sing about lately has been happening to me. I have lost my wife, friends, and I'm broke, plus nothing seems to be going my way. I feel like everything I sing about is happening for real in my life." Prov. 23:7a **For as he thinks in his heart, so is he.**

I am happy to say that this singer did eventually become a man of faith in Christ. His life turned around when he gave Jesus reign. One of the reasons his life turned around was that he started to say and live by what the Lord said was truth and reality concerning his life. Prov. 18:21 **The tongue has the power of life and death, and**

those who love it will eat its fruit.

You might say, "It can't be that simple - just change the way we talk and express ourselves and our lives will change with it." Yes, I truly believe this to be a reality if we follow up our talk with our actions. The Lord instructs the weak to say that they are strong. Joel 3:10b **Let the weak say, I am strong.** Why would God want us to keep saying we were strong when we did not feel that way? So that we would eventually become strong in God.

God also admonishes us to say that we have been redeemed, delivered, and rescued from our enemy. Psalm 107:2 **Let the redeemed of the LORD proclaim that he has redeemed them from the power of the foe.** Why does God want us confessing His deliverance in our life? So that the truth of our God delivering us gets deep down within our spirit and we start to live a life believing in the willingness of God to help us and the love that God has for us.

If all that is coming out of your mouth on a continual basis is filthiness, negativity, oppressiveness, and blasphemies then you will be snared by the words of your mouth. As you live out of this crass and vulgar existence, the fruit of that lifestyle choice will be your reward. You cannot expect a bounty of good, healthy, and lush results in a garden from planting moldy, diseased, and bad seeds. It does not work in nature and will not work in your life. James 3:11 **Can both freshwater and salt water flow from the same spring?** You will become snared by the words of your own mouth.

We have to make a conscious choice to say and speak the words of life and words that give life. Psalm 91:2 **I will say of the LORD, "He is my refuge and my fortress; my God, in Him I will trust."** The psalmist makes a statement in this verse, "I will say of the Lord." I will use my mouth to say what God says about me. It is our choice to say what we say.

We have to make a declaration that we will become a source of blessing by the way we speak and help untangle the snares we have created with our mouth. We want to talk and express what God says about us. His words toward us are words of peace and forgiveness, but we have to accept it as truth and declare it plainly.

The choice is ours to make. We can speak

blessing or cursing. What fruit do you want in your life? Deut. 30:19 **This day I call the heavens and the earth as witnesses against you that I have set before you life and death, blessings and curses. Now choose life, so that you and your children may live.**

WORDS HEAL

Proverbs 16:24 Pleasant words are as an honeycomb, sweet to the soul, and health to the bones.

How often have you heard the right word at the right time and it was healing to your soul? Oh, how wonderful that blessed feeling is in our inner being. We have also experienced the opposite when we were hit right in the heart with a malicious statement that hurt to the very core of our humanity.

The power of words is significant enough to kill a person, or heal a person right where they are standing. Prov. 12:18 **There is that speaks like the piercings of a sword: but the tongue of the wise is health**.

Yes, you have the power to bring life through words that will cause a merry heart of health to be activated within a person. The result is a medication that cannot be bought with a pharmaceutical prescription. Prov. 17:22 **A merry heart does good like a medicine: but a broken**

spirit dries the bones.

A few years ago I had heard of a Japanese experiment where the scientists were speaking joyfully and harshly to different clusters of rice. The result of this was they were getting interesting results as to the conditions and quality of the rice clusters.

Better still, I spoke to my friend Romay who had used this experiment to teach her children how words, good or bad, could affect the inside of other children. This is Romay's account of how she used the rice experiment and what the results were.

We sanitized two glass jars by boiling them with their lids for ten minutes. At the same time, we made one batch of plain white rice. Then we put the rice in the jars and closed them up and labeled one with 'love, thankful, and kind,' and the other with 'hate, unthankful, and unkind'.

We then put the jars side by side. Throughout the coming days, we would speak to the rice in the jars with words directed as to the label's instructions on each jar. To the love rice, we said love words (in the language and cadence of a preschool aged child) like 'I want to play with you,'

'you're beautiful,' and so on. To the 'hate' rice we would say the opposite type of words. Periodically the jars were moved around - separating them - and repeating the rice experiment for the benefit of the children to see how words can have an effect in life.

After three weeks the hate rice started turning brown and slimy, while the love rice stayed white. Eventually, the hate rice turned to a sludgy black liquid. The white rice has always stayed fluffy, just like the first day. The amazing part of this word experiment is that after two and a half years the jars were found in the garage where they were forgotten. They were still the same! The hate jar of rancid rice had gotten worse; the love rice was still white and fluffy. Stunning how words can affect life. Prov. 18:21 **Death and life are in the power of the tongue: and they that love it shall eat the fruit thereof.**

After I heard this story, I thought of the verses in Romans that basically says that all of creation is waiting for mankind to get their act together so that healing can come to this earth. Rom. 8:21 **Because the creature itself also shall be delivered from the bondage of corruption**

into the glorious liberty of the children of God. 22 **For we know that the whole creation groans and travails in pain together until now.**

Farmers, horse and dog whisperers will give testimony as to the power of words in the recovery of wounded animals that have been beaten and screamed at with profanities. Prov. 12:10 **A righteous man regards the life of his beast: but the tender mercies of the wicked are cruel.** We can change the very environment we live in by speaking God's words within that environment.

When I hear words delivered in sarcasm or malice, I call it "shriking out." Shrikes are some of the smallest birds of prey in North America. The foods they eat include small rodents and other species of small birds. Shrikes are known for impaling their victims on thorn bushes and barbed wire fences, then tearing their prey apart piece by piece.

What a description of what we are doing to others when we use hurtful and sarcastic quips to make our all-important point. How many spouses, male or female, are eviscerated by the other's burning complaint or harsh dig? Our raison d'être as Christians should be to bring life with our God-given ability to speak healing words to each other and everyone we meet. Prov. 15:23 **A man hath joy by the answer of his mouth: and a word spoken in due season, how good is it!**

I want to be a healer in this world. If the starting point is my vocabulary with the right spirit behind it, then let my words be the words of kindness and peace for us all. Psalm 107:20 **He sent his word, and healed them, and delivered them from their destructions.**

NEED A PHARISECTOMY?

Proverbs 9:6 Forsake the foolish, and live; and go in the way of understanding.

Do you need a Pharisectomy? Will the Pharisectomy hurt? Only if you judge and malign others.

Pastor Peter Haas wrote a book *Pharisectomy: How to Joyfully Remove Your Inner Pharisee and other Religiously Transmitted Diseases.*

I heard a minister of the Gospel say, "The more that he turned toward grace and lived in its peaceful place, the more his Pharisaical attitude within him was cut away." He determined that he had received a Pharisectomy. Of course, I laughed when I heard him say it, but realised that I could give witness to the same thing.

The closer to grace that I live and believe, the Pharisee within me is cut off and my hypocrisy is actively dealt with. Matt. 23:13 **But woe unto you, scribes and Pharisees, hypocrites! for ye shut up the kingdom of heaven against men: for ye neither go in yourselves, neither suffer**

ye them that are entering to go in.

When I started to extend grace to everyone around me, I found it easier to acknowledge my own sin and shortcomings; therefore, I could joyfully repent of being judgemental. Rom. 14:13 **Let us not therefore judge one another any more: but judge this rather, that no man put a stumbling block or an occasion to fall in his brother's way.**

I find that when I offer grace from a non-criticising position, there is liberty and joy in my heart toward my brothers in the Lord. Even better is the closeness I feel in my relationship with Christ. Psalms 73:28 **But it is good for me to draw near to God: I have put my trust in the Lord GOD, that I may declare all thy works.**

It is the Pharisee and his traditions within us that stop the Word of God from having an effective result in our spiritual lives. Mark 7:13a **Making the word of God of none effect through your tradition.** We are unwilling to change our hearts toward God's leading, because we have been taught a tradition that is no longer working for us. Yet, we fight to keep this tradition because it is how we have always done it in the past.

I am not talking about a doctrinal principle of truth. It is when we say, "We have always done it that way in this church!" These traditions can become an Ishmael to us and hinder the move of God within us, because God is trying to get an Isaac born of vision into our hearts. Gen. 17:18 **And Abraham said unto God, O that Ishmael might live before thee!** 19 **And God said, Sarah thy wife shall bear thee a son indeed; and thou shalt call his name Isaac: and I will establish my covenant with him for an everlasting covenant, and with his seed after him.**

When I lived in Queensland, Australia, there was a particular grass that I loved to smell. The sun's heat would cause this grass to give off a sweet curry scent. The locals call it Molasses-Grass. The dairy farmers hate it, because if their cows eat this grass the milk will take on a spoiled taste.

The farmers are vigilant in keeping this grass out of their paddocks. We should be just as vigilant, through grace, in keeping the Pharisee out of our souls. If we do not evict this Pharisaical attitude, our religion will produce a spoiled taste for everyone in our lives. We need to cut the Pharisee right out of us.

We want the grace of our Lord to perfume and flow from our hearts, that we may represent Christ's salvation in the beauty of His love and truth. Will this transformation from the heart of a Pharisee hurt? Will we be able to forsake the foolishness in our lives? I thank my God that He is not finished with us. He is working to bring us into His fullness. Jude 1:24 **Now unto Him that is able to keep you from falling, and to present you faultless before the presence of His glory with exceeding joy.** Amen and amen!

VERITAS: TRUTHFUL, GENUINE

Proverbs 22:12 The eyes of the LORD preserve knowledge, and He overthrows the words of the transgressor.

We do not have to worry about anything the transgressor says, because his words have no power or value. God will overthrow the words of the enemy with the word of God that lives forever and abides within us. The words of the enemy are often loud, vulgar, and threatening but the word of God has power, life, long-suffering, and love.

The words of the transgressor are hopeless, uninspiring, and devoid of fulfillment while promoting lack. The words of the enemy are lawless and full of subterfuge, always trying to cut down those who know Jesus Christ. It's a one trick pony designed to leave one wanting.

Jesus specialized in words of power, love, and faith. The Lord was and is constantly encouraging us to speak the way God speaks when it comes to the love relationship we have with Him. It truly matters who we believe we are in Christ. We are expected to believe our born-again righteousness and speak out by faith and humility who Christ has made us in this life.

There are things that God says about us that we have to come to grips with and start believing is true and genuine. The angels of God, who are our servants, are waiting to hear the word of God come from our hearts so that they may act upon God's words to bring glory to God and bring the Kingdom of God into our very homes and victory into our lives. Psalm 103:20 **Bless the LORD, ye his angels, that excel in strength, that do his commandments, hearkening unto the voice of his word.**

We are a new creation because of the blood of our Savior Jesus. 2Cor. 5:17 **Therefore if any man be in Christ, he is a new creature: old things are passed away; behold, all things are become new.** All things have become new and available to us because we have been loved into an eternal relationship with our God. Now we are expected to take on the relationship of sons. Sons who talk like their heavenly Father.

The word of God says we are clean. John 15:3

Now ye are clean through the word which I have spoken unto you. We then should say, "We are clean." The word of God says we are the salt of the earth. Matt. 5:13a **Ye are the salt of the earth.** We are the preservers of life and should say so. The word of God says we are the light of the world. Matt. 5:14a **Ye are the light of the world.** We are to let the brilliance of Christ shine in what we say and do.

The word of God says we are friends with Christ. John 15:15a **Henceforth I call you not servants; for the servant knows not what his lord does: but I have called you friends.** If God says we are His friends, then friends we are. The word of God says we are heirs of God Himself. Titus 3:7 **That being justified by his grace, we should be made heirs according to the hope of eternal life.** We should confess our inheritance in Christ and give thanks because it is so.

The word of God says we are chosen, royalty, holy, and special. 1Pet. 2:9 **But ye are a chosen generation, a royal priesthood, an holy nation, a peculiar people; that ye should shew forth the praises of him who hath called you out of**

darkness into his marvellous light.

Should I go on and mention that we are God's sons, daughters, elect, ambassadors, brothers, the temple of the Holy Spirit, children of God, and the beloved? To top it off, we are kings and priests created through the new birth to minister to God and to rule with righteousness in His kingdom here on earth. Rev. 1:6 **And hath made us kings and priests unto God and His Father; to Him be glory and dominion for ever and ever. Amen.**

When are we going to start saying what God says we should say and be in the glorious kingdom of our Lord and Savior? All these blessings will help change our character because of what God has done for us through the acceptable sacrifice Jesus offered for all of us. Wow!! What more can I say but "Wow!!"

When we are being who God says we are in Him, then we are being truthful and genuine. God says that we are more than conquerors. Would God lie to us? No! Num. 23:19 **God is not a man, that he should lie; neither the son of man, that he should repent: hath he said, and shall he not do it? or hath he spoken, and**

shall he not make it good?

We are who God says we are by faith, and we have what God says we have. There is no philosophical debate on this truth. It is what the Lord says it is. Stop listening to the words of the transgressor who has nothing victorious for us to hang our heart on. Our being is in Christ. What He accomplished is ours to have and to dispense to a lost world. Acts 17:28 **For in him we live, and move, and have our being; as certain also of your own poets have said, For we are also his offspring.**

Confessing what God has asked us to say about ourselves is obedience and brings pleasure to God's heart. Why not start by confessing our righteousness, since God says we are His righteousness through Christ. I think God would like that.

Everyone, say it together, **"For he hath made Him to be sin for us, who knew no sin; that we might be made the righteousness of God in Him."** Now, didn't that feel good? Blessings. Psalm 12:6 **The words of the LORD are pure words: as silver tried in a furnace of earth, purified seven times.**

FIRST NAME BASIS

Proverbs 8:17 I love those who love me, and those who seek me find me.

I was talking with a friend who was concerned about her husband's fears and uncertainty for the future. She felt he was too focused on all the things that are missing in his life right now. I had to remind her that she was a born-again child of the living God and her husband had not stepped into that relationship yet. Her relationship with God is on a first name basis.

When the Lord talks to her, He calls her by her name. She responds in like manner saying, "Yahweh, Jehovah, or Jesus." Her husband, however, is living and trying to access life from the position of an outsider. He is looking in on what God is perceived to be. He may not have the assurance his wife has in her faith, because she knows her God personally. Dan. 11:32b **But the people who know their God will display strength and take action.**

This is one of the most amazing and fantastic

things that happens to an individual who becomes a blood-washed child of the living God. We, who know our God, have the opportunity to come into a relationship with our heavenly Father through Jesus Christ. We become children who are known on a first name basis. Rom. 8:15 **So you have not received a spirit that makes you fearful slaves. Instead, you received God's Spirit when he adopted you as his own children. Now we call him, "Abba, Father."** This is a hard concept for many to accept. It must be done by faith in Christ and the belief that God is initiating this covenant relationship.

God knows us by name. We also know Him by name. We will spend an eternity finding out the depths of all the Lord's name because of the infinite nature of our God. He will always be approachable throughout eternity and will forever reveal the full beauty of all the meanings and riches of His name. The name God wants us to know and love is the name of Jesus. For God has exalted His name above every name that is named. Phil. 2:9 **Therefore, God elevated him to the place of highest honor and gave him the name above all other names,** 10 **that at**

the name of Jesus every knee should bow, in heaven and on earth and under the earth, 11 **and every tongue confess that Jesus Christ is Lord, to the glory of God the Father.** It does not get much plainer than that. Jesus is the name to know. Know it intimately and receive it by faith.

Friendship with God is possible and actually expected from God's point of view. James 2:23 **And the Scripture was fulfilled, saying, "And Abraham believed God, and it was counted to him for righteousness," and he was called a friend of God.** Jesus made a remark that expressed friendship was the relationship He desired. John 15:15 **I no longer call you servants, because a servant does not know his master's business. Instead, I have called you friends, for everything that I learned from my Father I have made known to you.** What an awesome thought that God wants friendship with all those He has created.

Through the cross and the blood of Jesus Christ, God has made it possible for every living person on earth to enter into a loving friendship with the All Mighty God of the universe. Think about how overwhelming it would be if we were trying to get to God on our own good works. The pressure would be too great to handle. We would end up ruled by a religious self-righteousness and full of doubts. God's gift of friendship is righteous and already done for us. We just have to say, "Yes, Lord, I accept your gift of eternal life through Jesus our Lord."

Psalm 103:14 **For He knows how we are formed, He remembers that we are dust.** Only a God who knows our frame and humanity can reach out and create a way of salvation that brings us ever closer to His Majesty and loving heart. Wow, God knows my name. I can call Him anytime, whether my life is going well or seems misdirected. I can count on His perfect love for me to guide me back to His side where I can say, "Jesus, you are so good to me," and hear the Lord say, "I love you, Norm." Wow! Count me in that blessing any day. Prov. 8:17 **I love those who love me, and those who seek me find me.**

PART FIVE:

QUESTIONS FOR UNDERSTANDING

1. *What did you learn in this section of the book?*
2. *What surprised you the most?*
3. *What subject(s) spoke to your heart?*
4. *Did the material that you read help you understand the subject(s) more or less?*
5. *What topics are important to you? Why?*
6. *How do these articles relate to you?*
7. *After reading this section of the book, what will you change in your life?*

BENEDICTION

Heavenly Father, please bless all the readers who have taken the time to read this book. May the Lord's face shine on each one of them and give them the desires of their hearts.

Through lessons gleaned from each chapter, enable them to overcome all the attacks of the enemy. Remind them in the midst of their battles that Christ has made us overcomers in this life.

May recall knowledge of the scriptures they read fill them with peace.

May God direct them to accomplish all God has for them, and may everyone be fulfiled. In Jesus name!

ABOUT THE AUTHOR

I have been in Christian ministry in one form or another for over forty years. I attended Commonwealth Bible College in Katoomba, New South Wales, Australia, in 1980. Ministry at that time involved prison ministries, preaching on the radio in a small town, and church-related works of all kinds. I have taught bible college courses and also have been involved in personal discipleship training. God has blessed me all along the way. Now I have the opportunity to write down what was experienced throughout the years. The Lord has blessed me with sound and forthright material to write a series of Christian devotionals.

I have lived the testimonies on these pages and can attest to the fact that God is so faithful and good. My hope is that your soul will be enriched as you read this book. God bless you.

CONNECT WITH NORM

Norm's Blog can now be found online in English, French and Spanish.

Your comments on any of the hundreds of blog posts are appreciated.

English sirnorm.com

French sirnorm.com/fr/

Spanish sirnorm.com/es/

www.ingramcontent.com/pod-product-compliance
Lightning Source LLC
Chambersburg PA
CBHW070347090426
42733CB00009B/1317

9781988226460